BFI FILM CLASSICS

. . . .

Edward Buscombe
SERIES EDITOR

Cinema is a fragile medium. Many of the great classic films of the past now exist, if at all, in damaged or incomplete prints. Concerned about the deterioration in the physical state of our film heritage, the National Film Archive, a Division of the British Film Institute, has compiled a list of 360 key films in the history of the cinema. The long-term goal of the Archive is to build a collection of perfect showprints of these films, which will then be screened regularly at the Museum of the Moving Image in London in a year-round repertory.

BFI Publishing has now commissioned a series of books to stand alongside these titles. Authors, including film critics and scholars, film-makers, novelists, historians and those distinguished in the arts, have been invited to write on a film of their choice, drawn from the Archive's list. Each volume will present the author's own insights into the chosen film, together with a brief production history and a detailed filmography, notes and bibliography. The numerous illustrations have been specially made from the Archive's own prints.

With new titles published each year, the BFI Film Classics series will rapidly grow into an authoritative and highly readable guide to the great films of world cinema.

Publicity still of Glenn Ford and Gloria Grahame

BFI FILM CLASSICS

THE BIG HEAT

Colin McArthur

BFI PUBLISHING

First published in 1992 by the
BRITISH FILM INSTITUTE
21 Stephen Street, London W1P 1PL

British Library Cataloguing in Publication Data

McArthur, Colin
The Big Heat
I. Title
791.4372

ISBN 0–85170–342–9

Designed by
Andrew Barron & Collis Clements Associates

Typesetting by
Fakenham Photosetting Limited, Norfolk

Printed in Great Britain by
The Trinity Press, Worcester

CONTENTS

IN MEMORIAM

Bill McCumesty
(1934–1987)

ACKNOWLEDGMENTS

I am grateful to David Sharp and the staff of BFI Library and Information Services for obtaining from abroad materials relevant to *The Big Heat* and for servicing my research needs; to the staff of the BFI Stills, Posters and Designs Department for supplying stills; and to Ed Buscombe of BFI Publishing not only for sympathetic editing but for endorsing an approach to *The Big Heat* which goes far beyond the text of the film and its moment of production. Film credits were compiled by Markku Salmi.

Counterpoint: 'the bright, friendly world of the Bannion home . . .'
'. . . and the bleak world of The Retreat'.

INTRODUCTION

....

No doubt oversimplifying, I think of the first quarter century of my life as pre-intellectual. It was a time mainly of socialising, sport and massive consumption of cinema and other aspects of popular culture, with the grudging concessions to formal education the law required. My experience of cinema and popular culture over this period bred strong tastes which, on the whole, I did not much reflect on. Two cinematic experiences of that time remain vivid to this day. Somewhere around the age of fifteen I wandered into a rather seedy cinema in central Glasgow, one which showed foreign films for their alleged erotic, rather than artistic, qualities. A couple of hours later I came reeling out, profoundly shaken by the film I had just seen but quite unable to explain why. The film was Luis Buñuel's *Los Olvidados*.

Some years later, in 1954 to be precise, I was reaching the end of my national service in the Army in York. I went with some other soldiers to the cinema, quite a run-of-the-mill visit. Afterwards my friends were puzzled by my uncharacteristic silence and, when I did open up, my less than articulate enthusiasm for the film. It was, of course, *The Big Heat*. In both cases I was aware of being in the presence of exceptional films, but would have been hard-pressed to explain why they were, in their different ways, superb examples of cinema.

The next quarter century of my life was a period of intense intellectual activity relating to cinema and other aspects of popular culture. It wasn't until about sixteen years after initially seeing *The Big Heat* – at the point in British (film) culture when discussion of Hollywood, its *auteurs* and its genres was very much on the agenda – that I had the chance to begin to work out why it was such a remarkable movie. Some of these reflections surfaced in British Film Institute summer schools of the late 1960s and early 1970s and, more permanently, in my writings on the gangster movie, of which more below, at about the same time. However, such attention as I was able to give *The Big Heat* was within the much larger project of exploring the Hollywood crime movie and those *auteurs* who, it seemed to me, had realised the most striking examples of the genre.

This series of books offers the opportunity not just to look at *The Big Heat* itself, although Chapter 5 does precisely that to an extent the film deserves, but also to locate it in its moment of production and its subsequent resonance in the (film) culture.

Chapter 1 deals with William P. McGivern's original novel. This is a worthwhile exercise because, as well as having a close relationship with the finished film, the novel is an interesting artefact in its own right, not least for its unusually acute moral sense. Also, in the current reawakening of interest in the American crime novel, McGivern's work seems (as far as I am aware) to have been unjustly neglected.

Chapter 2 deals with Columbia Pictures' institutional involvement with *The Big Heat* from its acquisition as a *Saturday Evening Post* serial to its marketing as finished film. This chapter is very much concerned with the ethos of Columbia, Hollywood, the United States and its world position at this time, and how these are imprinted on *The Big Heat*.

Chapter 3 deals with one particular aspect of how the meaning of a film is constructed, the response of critics and reviewers. *The Big Heat* was released initially in Britain in 1954, then re-released in 1988. This chapter is particularly concerned with the vastly differing critical attitudes to the film at these points, and what this difference reveals about the social and cultural changes in Britain between 1954 and 1988.

Chapter 4 was in many ways the most difficult to write. It was originally conceived simply as a response to certain published critiques of my 1970s writings about Fritz Lang and *The Big Heat*, but the very act of going back to this time proved to be, as I say in the text, like opening a Pandora's Box. In the educational and critical milieu in which I spent most of my working life – the British Film Institute and the discourses and institutions which surround it – the act of film criticism was never solely a question of aesthetics. There were always at stake issues of (film) pedagogy and, ultimately, politics. Trying to extract critical attitudes to *The Big Heat* from this complex historical moment was, to change the metaphor, like trying to extricate one strand of spaghetti from a pot. Readers who find these questions tiresome, therefore, should be warned that Chapter 4 is as much about the pedagogies and politics of such institutions as the British Film Institute and the journal of film theory, *Screen*, as it is about critical methods relating to *The Big Heat*.

As the book as a whole demonstrates, awareness of *The Big Heat*, both as a popular cultural intertext and as a complex cinematic text, has increased since the 1950s. It is a recurrent assertion in this book that the act of criticism should be pedagogically and politically useful. The critical methods brought to bear on *The Big Heat* in Chapter 5 are primarily those which engage with narrative structure and cinematic *mise-en-scène*. Up to the early 1970s there was an indigenous British critical tradition (best exemplified by the practice of those critics associated with the journal *Movie*) which deployed these methods, particularly the latter. The eclipse of *Movie*, due partly to the hostility of *Screen*, was a great loss to British film culture. I hope that the form of analysis of *The Big Heat* offered here will have the pedagogical and political effect of reminding a new generation of film students of the *mise-en-scène* tradition of film criticism.

. . . .

An operational note. Certain parts of the text refer to Fritz Lang's papers in the Cinémathèque Française in Paris. Papers relating to *The Big Heat* are extensively referred to, and often reproduced in French translation, in Gérard Leblanc and Brigitte Devismes' *Le Double Scénario chez Fritz Lang*. I too quote from some of this material but, not having had access to the original English versions of Lang's papers in the Cinémathèque Française, I have had to retranslate the French versions into English. This note is by way of explanation of any disparities between the originals and my English retranslations of the French versions by Leblanc and Devismes.

1

....

'THE BIG HEAT' AS NOVEL

William P. McGivern's novel was published in 1952. The current critical interest in the American crime novel is heavily weighted towards the 'classic' crime writers of the pre-war period and the 1940s, such as Raymond Chandler, Dashiel Hammett and James M. Cain, although critical attention is beginning to be paid to younger writers such as George V. Higgins. The growing critical interest has prompted better factual documentation of the field in the form of guides and encyclopaedias and it is here, rather than in the critical writing proper, that one can learn something about McGivern and his work.

Several of his novels have been adapted for the screen (*Shield for Murder*, 1951; *Rogue Cop*, 1954; *Odds Against Tomorrow*, 1957); and he has been a screenwriter in Hollywood (*The Wrecking Crew*, 1969; *Brannigan*, 1975) and in television, writing regularly for the *Kojak* series over the period 1973–77. Taking *The Big Heat* and two of McGivern's other novels adapted for the screen, *Shield for Murder* and *Rogue Cop*, one could produce an *auteur* study which would centre on the theme of police corruption and the blurring of distinctions between legality and criminality, also a recurrent theme in the work of Fritz Lang, who was to direct the screen adaptation of *The Big Heat*. Unlike Lang, however, McGivern seems to display a profound (often explicitly Christian) moral concern about the capacity of people to pass from legality to criminality, decency to brutality.

The Big Heat as novel begins in the precinct station on a bleak, rainy night with several detectives from the homicide squad hanging around (only one of whom, Burke, survives by name in the film) and a young black man waiting to be interrogated about a murder. It is into this setting – the novel is strong on police procedure – that Mrs Deery's telephone call, announcing the suicide of her policeman husband, comes. Like the film, the novel allows the initiating incident of the plot, the suicide, to be talked about and 'taken on board' before it introduces its central character, Sergeant Dave Bannion:

> The double doors of the Homicide Bureau swung open and a
> young man in a damp trenchcoat came in ... He was a large wide-

shouldered man in his middle thirties, with tanned, even features and steady gray eyes. Standing alone he didn't seem particularly big; it was only when Burke, a tall man himself, strolled over beside him, that Bannion's size became apparent. He stood inches taller than Burke, and his two hundred and thirty pounds were evenly distributed on a huge, rangy frame.

Apart from the evocation of the bleak precinct station and the setting out of the procedure for dealing with police suicides, the opening scene of the novel has two functions: to suggest Bannion's immense physical power (it later emerges that he has been a Notre Dame All American footballer) and to signify his basic decency and commitment to legality. The latter is revealed in his relationship with the black man:

'I didn't kill nobody,' the Negro said, standing, his large, bony hands working spasmodically. His head turned, his eyes touched each face in the room, frightened, helpless, defiant.

'Sit down,' the uniformed cop said to him. Burke smiled pleasantly at Bannion. 'I could find out in ten little minutes if you'd just let ——.' He stopped at the look on Bannion's face. 'Okay, okay. It was just a stray thought,' he said, shrugging elaborately.

'There won't be any of that stuff on my shift,' Bannion said.

'Okay, *okay*,' Burke said.

Bannion walked over to the Negro, who seemed to sense that he had got a break of some kind. 'We just want the truth from you,' Bannion said. 'If you've done nothing wrong you've got nothing to worry about. But if you have we'll find it out. Remember that.'

The black man surfaces later in the novel, with Bannion visiting his home and talking with his family. He fulfils the role (occupied by the disabled Selma Parker character in the film) of giving Bannion the initial lead in his hunt for the men who killed his wife. The interesting question of why the black man and his milieu are absent from the film is addressed in the next chapter.

Bannion's visit to the scene of the cop's suicide is much more procedurally detailed than in the film. Unlike the film, the novel does not divulge right away the crookedness of Tom Deery and his wife, but it does offer a clue that there is a problem by making separate characters comment on the absence of a suicide note. In the novel, Bannion has a substantial interior life, mostly signified by the kinds of books he reads and what he thinks, feels and says about them. This theme is set in play in the course of Bannion's detailed examination of the contents of the room in which Tom Deery died:

> Bannion closed the drawers, after replacing everything as he had found it, and walked over and glanced at the volumes in the book cases. Most of them were in standard sets, history, biography, the novels of Scott and Dickens, and a selection of book club premiums.
>
> There was a shelf of travel books, he noticed, all of them well-worn. He picked out a couple of them and flipped through the pages, wondering idly at this bent of Deery's. There were pencilled notes in Deery's handwriting in the margins, and Bannion immediately became more interested. There was nothing more potentially revealing, he felt, than a man's honest, impulsive reactions to a book ...

As the analysis of the film in Chapter 5 reveals, one of its major structural oppositions is that between the world of crime and Bannion's home. This opposition is strong also in the novel:

> It had been a run-of-the-mill night, like a thousand he had known in the past. He felt comfortably tired as he followed the curving Schuylkil out to Germantown, listening with only mild interest to a news programme on the radio. It was good to be on his way home, he thought. Home to dinner, to Katie.

As with many of the words actually spoken in the novel, as opposed to the framing narrative discourses, the dialogue in the scene in the film in which the Bannion home is introduced is taken almost verbatim from the novel, evoking the friendly, bantering relationship between Bannion and his wife. What is absent in the novel are the various acts of sharing which the film shows. But, of course, the (purportedly) egalitarian relationship in the film is constructed in direct opposition to the series of hierarchical relationships, based on corrupt power and wealth, with which the film opens.

The domestic scene in the novel is also detailed about the kind of books Bannion reads, for it is primarily in relation to them that his moral consciousness is signified. Bannion is reflecting after dinner:

> Deery's travel books, tracked with marginal notes, was an odd thing. Why the devil did people read travel books? To learn something, to kill time, to escape into a world of armchair adventuring. All of these reasons, perhaps. Possibly Deery was simply bored, and used the books as a crutch to help him through the long evenings. Bannion smiled slightly and glanced at the bookcase beside his chair. There were his crutches then, comfortable well-worn ones, with pages as familiar to him as the lines of his hands. They were travel books of a sort; they were volumes of philosophy, and the world of ideas could be travelled and explored as well as foreign countries, and strange jungles. Deery read about the bullfighting in Spain, while he read the spiritual explosions of St John of the Cross, who was a Spaniard but no bullfighter. What was the difference? Why did one man read one thing, the next man another?. ... I read philosophy, he thought, because I'm too weak to stand up against the misery and meaningless heartbreak I run into every day on the job. I'm no scholar. I wouldn't touch Nietzsche or Schopenhauer with a ten-foot pole ... I don't want to listen to idols being smashed, I want to read something which puts sense into life. ... Deery, he thought, might have been better off with these books than with the descriptions of fertility charms in Pompeii. These were the men he had gone to himself for peace of mind. St John of the Cross, Kant, Spinoza, Santayana. The gentle philosophers, the ones who thought it was natural for man to be good, and that evil was the aberrant course, abnormal, accidental, out of line with man's true needs and nature.

Unlike many examples of the crime novel – the works of Mickey

Spillane come to mind – McGivern's novel is a profoundly *moral* work in the sense that it is concerned with the necessity of preserving standards of decency and legality in a meaningless universe. The passage quoted above comes close to stating the controlling idea of both novel and film.

The novel and film are most similar at the level of plot, with the events of the latter tracking those of the former quite closely: the bar girl Lucy Carroway's (Lucy Chapman in the film) call to Bannion's home querying the circumstances of Tom Deery's (Tom Duncan in the film) death; Bannion visiting her at the bar where she works, 'The Triangle' ('The Retreat' in the film); Bannion's second visit to Mrs Deery/Duncan; Bannion being reprimanded by his superior, Lieutenant Wilks, for bothering her; the discovery of Lucy's tortured body; Bannion's sense of guilt at not having taken her story more seriously; and Bannion's visit to Lagana's house. Certain changes in the way the film deals with these events can be explained partly by the film censorship conventions of the time: the suppression of Lucy's account of Mrs Deery/Duncan's feigned pregnancies; references to drug-taking and drug-dealing; and Bannion contemplating Lucy's tortured and murdered body on a slab in the county morgue – a scene which, if the film had been made from the late 1960s on, would almost certainly have been shown on screen.

The main difference between novel and film, however, is the narrative condensation the film imposes on these events and the paring down of the number of characters involved. In keeping with the novel's representation of police work as dogged routine and procedure, the events in the novel extend over several chapters and involve slow, painstaking investigation of the circumstances surrounding Deery/Duncan's suicide and Lucy's disappearance. Also present in the novel are several characters absent from or only vestigially present in the film, and 'The Triangle', although seedy and threadbare, does not have the force 'The Retreat' has of being at the centre of a web of violence and corruption. In the novel, throughout these events, Bannion has substantial relationships with several characters who do not appear in the film: Parnell, the county detective; Furnham, a newspaperman who hangs round the precinct office; and Inspector Cranston, the single unblemished figure in the upper echelons of the police department. In the film this figure is merged with that of Wilks, totally corrupt in the novel, to produce a highly ambiguous figure, semi-corrupt though ultimately straight. The period covered by these events in the novel is also dominated by a criminal, Biggie Burrows, who does not appear but who, Bannion establishes, has been seen escorting Lucy out of town. Much of the action is concerned with establishing Burrows' background and appearance and tracking his movements, in fact tracking an absence.

Because of the procedural detail which forms a core of interest in the novel, the blowing-up of Katie Bannion by a car bomb meant for Bannion himself comes closer to the centre of the novel rather than about a third of the way in, as with the film. The closing up of the marital home, Bannion's quitting the police and becoming an avenger rather than an investigator, and his inhabiting the soulless world of those he hunts, are all present in both novel and film, Bannion's moral decline in the former being signified primarily through his changing relationship with his books. Where the film has to rely on milieu (the Bannion home is completely bare of furniture) and the actor's performance, the novel can use milieu and Bannion's interior life to chart the change in him:

> Bannion stood in the front room, his hands in his overcoat pockets, glancing about for the last time. There was nothing else to hold him here. ...
>
> He dropped his keys on the coffee table, and then looked around again, at the imitation fireplace, the mantel, bare of pictures now, at the radio, liquor cabinet, at the sofa where she had usually sat to read, and at his own big chair. It was a room he had known by heart, but it was strange and unfamiliar to him now, as impersonal as a furniture arrangement in a shop window. It was a clean and silent room in a clean and silent apartment and he looked at it without any feeling at all.
>
> He glanced once at his books beside his chair, his old, familiar companions. He wasn't taking them with him, Hume, Locke, Kant, the men who had struggled and attacked the problems of living through all their lives. What could they tell him now of life? He knew the answers, and the knowledge was a dead, cold weight in his heart. Life was love; not love of God,

love of Humanity, love of Justice, but love of one other person. When that love was destroyed, you were dead too.

Bannion's priest prevails upon him to take just one book with him, *The Ascent of Mount Carmel* by St John of the Cross, but when he reaches the anonymous hotel room which, as avenger, will be his home, he throws it contemptuously in a corner. But since the controlling idea of the novel (and the film) is that there is a line between good and evil, criminality and legality, which should not be crossed, the narrative has to bring Bannion back from the pit of vengeful hatred into which he has sunk. This is orchestrated, in the novel, by the rallying of many of the characters to his aid, particularly after the corrupt police department takes the guard off his brother-in-law's house, where his young daughter is living, thus exposing her to kidnap by the mob. Parnell, the county detective, helps; Bannion's brother-in-law replaces the withdrawn police by a posse of his ex-Army buddies; Inspector Cranston stands guard outside the house; and even Bannion's priest shows up. It is this which begins to rehumanise Bannion.

> Bannion walked to his car and slid in behind the wheel, feeling something other than hate inside him for the first time since Katie had been murdered.

The process of Bannion's rehumanising can be tracked by comparing the way he deals with Larry Smith and the way he deals with Mrs Deery. In the film (see below) the scenes are mounted in precisely the same way, as acts of near-strangulation. This is the way he deals with Larry Smith in the novel:

> Bannion's hands shot out, terrible hands on the end of long, powerful arms, and closed relentlessly about Larry's throat. ... Larry raised his head slowly. Bannion loomed above him, pitiless and terrible ...

Having induced Larry to talk, this avenging angel figure (as in the film) signs his death warrant:

> 'You're through, little man,' Bannion said in a low voice. 'I'm

Two acts of near-strangulation: Larry . . .
. . . and Bertha Duncan

> going to spread the word that you talked. Stone will know in an
> hour, Lagana five minutes later. You picked the wrong racket,
> little man. You might have been a happy book keeper. Now
> you'll never have the chance.'

In the film, the strangulation of Bertha Duncan (Mrs Deery) is
prevented only by the intervention of the police. In the novel it is rather
different, reminiscent of Bannion's final encounter with Vince Stone
(Max Stone in the novel) in the film, and involves a gun rather than
strangulation. As Bannion points the gun at her:

> This was the end of it, Bannion thought, seeing her as only the
> last obstacle between him and vengeance. When the shot
> sounded, when this mute, foolishly gesticulating creature was
> dead, he would put his gun away. The job would be done. ...
> Why did he wait? He had only to pull the trigger, let the firing pin
> snap forward, and the steel-jacketed bullet would take care of this
> soft, perfumed, sadistic bitch, and with her Stone, Lagana, the
> hoodlums who had murdered his wife and held this town in their
> big, bitter grip. ... Why did he wait? They had killed, why
> shouldn't he? They had murdered Lucy Carroway, Kate, his life
> and love, as they'd destroy bothersome insects. Why should he
> bind himself with morals which they had mocked? ...
>
> Bannion's arm came slowly down with the muzzle of the
> gun pointed at the floor. 'I don't have the right to kill you,' he
> said, in a low, raging voice.

In both novel and film, Bannion's rehumanising is tracked through his
relationship with Debby Ward (Debby Marsh in the film). Stone's girl,
she flees to Bannion's hotel room when Stone scalds her face with
coffee. The novel is much less ambiguous than the film on a number of
aspects of the relationship. It is not clear in the film if Bannion is
attracted to Debby. Stone scalds her because she has gone to Bannion's
hotel with him, she to seduce him, he primarily to pump her for
information about his wife's killers. More ambiguous is whether he is
sexually attracted to her. There is no doubt in the novel:

> 'Do you really want me to go?' she said, turning at the door and

coming close to him, so close that the points of her small, firm breasts touched the rough fabric of his jacket.

'You're Stone's girl,' Bannion said, dropping his hand from her arm. He felt disgusted with himself, betrayed and shaken by his need. 'I wouldn't touch anything of Stone's with a ten foot pole.' ...

Bannion slammed the door on her and then stood with his back to it and stared bitterly at the small, soft indentation her body had made in his bed.

There is a strong suggestion in the way the film is put together that Bannion, consciously or unconsciously, cedes his impulse to kill Bertha Duncan to Debby. There is no such implication in the novel. After his abortive attempt to kill Mrs Deery, Bannion talks with Debby on the telephone:

'How did your lead turn out?'

He sighed. 'A dead end street. This will be Greek to you, but one of our city's finest left a note and then blew a hole through his head. The note will do what I may never be able to do to Lagana and company. It will be his end. However, Deery's wife has the note now, and I wasn't tough enough to bend the Fifth Commandment even a little bit. If I had – well that's another story. Don't worry about it, Debby. There'll be another chance.'

'You sound cryptic, if that's the right word,' Debbie said.

'Don't worry about it,' he said. He had talked only to relieve the pressure inside him, but it hadn't helped.

Having given Debby the information about the suicide note which will give her the motivation to kill Mrs Deery, Bannion is then exculpated by the framing narrative discourse, the authorial voice, which tells the reader that he had no ulterior motive in giving this information to Debby but 'talked only to relieve the pressure inside him.' As will be shown, the film is infinitely more complex on this question.

The plot resolutions of the novel are rather different from those of the film. In the film Lagana is indicted, in the novel he dies of a heart attack; in the film Stone, scalded by Debby, is then arrested, in the novel he is shot down in the street; in the film Debby is shot by Stone; in the novel, having killed Mrs Deery, she shoots herself. In both film and novel, however, her death scene is the occasion of Bannion's full reintegration into humanity through being able to talk to Debby about his life with Katie. In the novel, since Bannion's humanity and slippage from it have been signified most centrally through his relationship with his books, it is through this relationship that his return to humanity is recorded. As, in the early morning light, he walks away from the hospital where Debby has just died:

> The milk wagon in the next block was moving, and the clopping ring of the horses' hooves was a pleasant and familiar sound in the stillness....
> 'My house being now at rest.' The lines of St John came to Bannion unconsciously, and they seemed as fresh as the day he had first read them.... Something had ended this morning, he knew. Now he was starting over, not with hatred but only with sadness.
> That wasn't too bad, he thought.

As we shall see, the ending of the film is altogether more ambiguous.

2
....
ENTER COLUMBIA PICTURES

Soon after publication *The Big Heat* was serialised in the *Saturday Evening Post*, the seven parts running from December 1952 to February 1953. Serials from mass circulation journals like the *Post* and *Collier's Magazine* were important sources of Hollywood adaptations. The famous Anthony Mann/James Stewart Western, *The Man from Laramie*, was picked up from the same source about this time. A brief paragraph in the *Hollywood Reporter* (the main trade daily for news about production plans and developing projects) of 12 January 1953 indicates that *The Big Heat* had been purchased by Columbia and that Robert Arthur would produce the film. The wider production and film-industrial context of the time help explain the picture which will emerge of *The Big Heat* as a modest production in no way regarded as out of the ordinary by Columbia itself or by the wider Hollywood film culture which, at the time, had other things on its mind.

The Hollywood film industry had emerged buoyant from World War 2, rising to a peak in 1946 when there were over ninety million admissions to cinemas every week. Thereafter, there began a decline, especially precipitous in the years 1947 to 1953. According to *Variety*, corporate profits in the motion picture industry fell from $187 million in 1948 to just $31 million in 1952. Several factors have been adduced to explain this decline: the post-war rise in the birth rate, tending to immobilise at home an important sector of the industry's traditional catchment age group; demographic changes which saw younger families moving from the inner cities to the suburbs; alterations in the patterns of spending whereby money that might formerly have financed several visits per week to the cinema went now towards a new house or automobile; and, not least, increased competition from radio and the rapidly developing medium of television. Indeed, the fact that the police series *Dragnet* was topping the television ratings in 1953 may have been a factor in Columbia's purchase of McGivern's novel.

At the moment that *The Big Heat* was going into production, therefore, Hollywood was a frightened industry economically. It was also frightened politically in that the House Committee on Un-American Activities had not yet lost interest in Hollywood. This is probably not greatly relevant to *The Big Heat*, although certain repressions which occurred in the transition from novel to screen (for instance, the elimination of all black characters and a reference to a left-wing trade union official) may have been due to political cautiousness. But the elimination of the black characters in *The Big Heat* may be more the result of generic factors. Many of Hollywood's most politically radical personnel were associated with films which foregrounded the plight of ethnic minorities, and at least one black actor (James Edwards) had his career damaged by his refusal to testify against Paul Robeson. But another black actor, Sidney Poitier, was building a career in such films as *No Way Out* (1950), *Cry the Beloved Country* (1952) and *The Blackboard Jungle* (1955). Blacks, it seems, could appear in 'problem' pictures, musicals, movies about sport, war movies, movies set in other countries. But, with the exception of the Harry Belafonte character in

Odds Against Tomorrow (1959), it is difficult to recall any black character in an American gangster movie prior to the cycle of 'blaxploitation' crime movies of the early 1970s initiated by *Shaft* (1971).

There is in Chapter 5 a discussion of the celebrated opening shot of the film, a close-up of a police .38 which is then taken out of frame to be used in a suicide. There was much discussion of this scene in the pre-production phase, with producer Robert Arthur indicating that the Production Code Administration, the Hollywood censorship mechanism, had expressed disquiet about the scene as written. It is quite likely that this discussion also relates to the wider context within which *The Big Heat* was being made. The *New York Times* reported in April 1953 that, for quite some time, the State Department had been receiving representations from foreign governments about the amount and quality of violence in American films imported to their countries. It seems that Sweden had been most vociferous in its complaints but that Australia, the United Kingdom, India and Indonesia had also made their views known. Clearly this would have been passed down the line from the State Department for two reasons. Too much or too graphic

The celebrated opening shot of the suicide gun

violence might be damaging economically in that offending films might be restricted to particular age groups (*The Big Heat* had an 'X' Certificate in Britain, the most restricted of all the censorship categories at the time). But it might also be damaging politically to the 'hearts and minds' campaign which the State Department, and other US agencies, were waging in the rapidly escalating Cold War.

Clearly, then, a number of factors impinged on the production context of *The Big Heat*, but the most pressing would undoubtedly have been the plummeting box-office returns on the American domestic scene. Columbia had perhaps less need to be economically afraid than most. The Depression of the 1930s was a severe setback to most of the film studios. Only two of them, Loew's/MGM and Columbia, were able to sustain profit growth throughout this period, the former through sheer corporate strength and the latter by concentrating on low-budget productions and developing a 'cheese-paring' corporate ethos for which it never lost the reputation. Among the major studios, Columbia always had the lowest salaries. In 1947, for instance, the year in which Louis B. Mayer earned $755,840, Harry Cohn, head of Columbia, earned $197,000. Unlike some other studios, Columbia never actually *lost* money, at least not until the Cohn brothers had ceased to be associated with the company in the late 1950s.

At the moment *The Big Heat* was going into production, Hollywood was reorganising itself to take account of the changes in (primarily) American social life and their effects on the industry's profitability. Some aspects of this reorganisation involved the shedding of labour – the winding-up of long-term contracts for stars, producers and other key personnel, and increased reliance on independent production packages. But it is Hollywood's response to television which helped push *The Big Heat* into the background, to confirm its low profile as a run-of-the-mill production. Characteristically, Columbia had seen not only danger but opportunity in the rise of television. As early as 1952 Ralph Cohn, Harry's son, had set up a television subsidiary, Screen Gems, to produce thirty-nine Ford Theater programmes, short television dramas sponsored by the Ford Motor Company. Columbia also took the lead in selling off its back library to television. But the best remembered Hollywood responses to television are the twin developments of CinemaScope and 3-D. During the period that *The Big Heat* moved through the production and distribution process, journals of comment on Hollywood affairs were dominated by these new technical processes. CinemaScope was, for technical reasons, able decisively to defeat its rival, with 20th Century-Fox's *The Robe*, the first CinemaScope feature production, generating enormous publicity and, in its advertising, putting paid to the threat from its erstwhile rival – 'a three-D effect . . . without glasses'.

Thus the wider economic context of Hollywood and the spectacular arrival of new technologies conspired to lower the profile of *The Big Heat*. But so too did the hierarchy within Columbia itself. Columbia had bought James Jones's blockbuster novel *From Here to Eternity*, and it is clear from the amount of activity the Columbia publicity machine put into pre-selling the resulting film (as well as its long shooting schedule and large budget) that it was going to be Columbia's 'big picture' of 1953.

The Big Heat's modest profile, as well as what the film trade considered important about the building of the project, is apparent from the following entries in the *Hollywood Reporter* over the period of the film's germination:

> *12 January 1953*: Announcement of *The Big Heat*'s purchase and that Robert Arthur will produce.
>
> *20 February*: Announcement that Glenn Ford will star, Fritz Lang direct and that the film will start 'rolling next week'.
>
> *3 March*: Announcement of Jocelyn Brando's casting and that the film 'rolls March 17'.
>
> *4 March*: Announcement of Gloria Grahame's casting.
>
> *10 March*: Announcement of Jean Louis as costume designer.
>
> *20 March*: *The Big Heat* recorded as having been in production for six days.
>
> *10 April*: *The Big Heat* recorded as having been in production for twenty-four days. (This is the last entry for the picture in the *Hollywood Reporter*'s production schedules.)

Gérard Leblanc and Brigitte Devismes' *Le Double Scénario chez Fritz Lang* (Paris, 1991), which draws on Lang's papers in the Cinémathèque Française, shows the extent to which Lang was revising

Sydney Boehm's first scenario up to and during the shooting of the film and was, in a sense, 'rewriting' it once more by the nature of his *mise-en-scène*, by the way he deployed all the resources of the cinema (acting, lighting, editing, sound, etc) in the process of shooting. This is the 'double scenario' referred to in the title of the book. Leblanc and Devismes had access to Boehm's original scenario (dated 20 January), to several revisions and emendations, and to the final shooting script (complete with annotations in Lang's own hand) as well as to several internal Columbia letters and memos which indicate input to the construction of the script/film from executive producer Jerry Wald and the concern of producer Robert Arthur about the handling of the opening suicide scene. Leblanc and Devismes record *The Big Heat* as being shot in twenty-eight days between 17 March and 15 April 1953.

Both the findings of Leblanc and Devismes and the information in the *Hollywood Reporter* point to several things. Most obviously, the period between the announcement of the book's purchase (12 January) and shooting being completed (15 April) seems astonishingly short, perhaps further confirming the run-of-the-mill quality of *The Big Heat*

Fritz Lang and Glenn Ford examine the rushes

in Columbia's production schedules. Also, if the book was purchased about 12 January and shooting began on 17 March (or 14 March according to Leblanc and Devismes), Sydney Boehm (incidentally, not deigned a mention in the *Hollywood Reporter*) must have been hired, have drafted (according to the evidence cited by Leblanc and Devismes, by 20 January), redrafted and had the script approved, all within two months. Likewise, if Fritz Lang (according to the *Hollywood Reporter*) joined the project around 20 February, he had about three weeks to make his own contribution to the script and rehearse with the principal players, some of whom were cast only days before shooting began. Reportedly, one of the principals, Lee Marvin, was simultaneously working on another Columbia picture, *The Wild One*.

The low profile of *The Big Heat*'s production continued with its release. Leblanc and Devismes had access to the report of a preview which took place at the Paradise Theater on the evening of 7 August 1953. There seem to have been two screenings, after which the audiences were asked to give responses within the categories Excellent, Good and Fair. Audience responses at the two screenings were:

	1	2
Excellent	105	151
Good	37	64
Fair	6	9

Asked about their responses to the actors, the audiences showed a marked enthusiasm for Glenn Ford and Gloria Grahame, who were foregrounded in the subsequent advertising of the film.

The pattern of the film's release and its box-office performance can be reconstructed from references in the *Motion Picture Herald*, the journal of film exhibitors. There is a trade review in the issue of 26 September 1953 and a release date of October 1953 is mentioned, which suggests that Columbia were in no particular hurry to get the film out. *From Here to Eternity*, for example, had already been released. In a *Motion Picture Herald* review, the voice is that of an exhibitor talking to other exhibitors, the aim being to tell them how the picture is likely to do in their theatres. There is a classificatory scheme with the categories Superior, Excellent, Very Good, Good, Average and Fair, as well as a Legion of Decency (the Roman Catholic pressure group) classification

in which the categories are A1, A2 and B. The review regards *The Big
Heat*'s business prospects as 'Good' – somewhat at odds with the
excellent results of the preview screenings – and it receives the Legion
of Decency's lowest rating of B. The *Motion Picture Herald*'s reviewer
would seem to have had a good eye for a film's prospects. The table
below is reproduced from the issue of 8 May 1954, the last week of *The
Big Heat*'s initial release run:

	EX	AA	AV	BA	PR
Back to God's Country (U-I)	1	23	45	18	6
Bad for Each Other (Col.)	–	–	2	8	5
Beachhead (UA)	–	6	9	3	1
Beat the Devil (UA)	18	–	2	8	9
Beneath the 12-Mile Reef (20th-Fox)	26	13	10	4	1
Best Years of Our Lives (RKO) (Reissue)	1	–	1	1	3
*Big Heat (Col.)	1	21	32	16	6
Bigamist, The (Filmakers)	–	1	7	–	6
Border River (U-I)	–	11	26	10	3
Botany Bay (Para.)	–	2	41	37	9
Boy from Oklahoma (WB)	20	15	20	11	6

Section from *Motion Picture Herald*'s table of Film Buyers Ratings, 8 May 1954.
EX means Excellent; AA Above Average; AV Average; BA Below Average;
PR Poor.

The Big Heat's pretty average box-office performance is borne out
by other indices of popularity, both among film workers and audiences.
It did not figure in the Academy Award nominations for 1953, unlike
Columbia's major project of that year, *From Here to Eternity*, which won
the categories of Best Picture, Best Director (Fred Zinnemann), Best
Supporting Actor (Frank Sinatra) and Best Supporting Actress (Donna
Reed). Nor did *The Big Heat* appear in the fan magazine *Photoplay*'s list
of the ten most popular pictures of the year. Top of that list too was
From Here to Eternity.

What all this reveals is an industry which regarded itself as
conceiving and delivering a modest picture, a view with which
audiences seemed to concur. But it is also clear that the same industry,
in part at least, *constructs* audience response by the way it markets a film.

Another mechanism in the construction of audience perception of a film is the press. What did critics and reviewers think of *The Big Heat* on its release?

3
....
(RE)CONSTRUCTING 'THE BIG HEAT'

The impression that Columbia, and American film culture in general, saw *The Big Heat* as a not very important picture is confirmed by its British release in May 1954, though this might be attributable not only to Columbia's lack of enthusiasm in promoting the film, but also to the peculiar nature of British film culture at the time and, in particular, its attitudes to Hollywood cinema. *The Big Heat* seems scarcely to have been reviewed at all in the general press in Britain. Only two such reviews survive in the British Film Institute's documentation collection, one from the *Jewish Chronicle*, the other from the *Sunday Times*. The latter, as well as indicating the particular tastes of the critic Dilys Powell, is not uncharacteristic of British film critics' attitudes to Hollywood at the time.

> Fritz Lang's gangster film ... is well worth looking at for those with the stomach for violence (it has an 'X' Certificate); exciting, made with cold, savage skill, played for all it is worth by Glenn Ford and Gloria Grahame.
> (9 May 1954)

The relative lack of importance accorded to Hollywood in the cinematic firmament of British reviewers is indicated not only by the brevity of the review, but in the attitude which saw Hollywood films as, at best, interestingly craftsmanlike ('cold, savage skill', 'played for all its worth').

The reviews in the specialised film press, while broadly within the same set of ideas about Hollywood, are rather more interesting. The *Monthly Film Bulletin*'s review is signed 'P.H.' (probably Penelope Houston):

> ... In its stereotyped way, the story of crime and administrative

corruption is slickly written and directed, although Fritz Lang
seems to have lost some of his old power to sustain dramatic
tension. The playing is generally adequate, with a showily
effective performance from Gloria Grahame. ... But though a
sequence such as the murder of Bannion's wife generates a certain
authentic shock effect, the main impression left by the film is of
violence employed arbitrarily, mechanically and in the long run
pointlessly.   (*MFB* no. 243, 1954)

Echoing the characteristic reticence of British reviewers regarding
cinematic violence ('good taste' was a cardinal value of this most
bourgeois of milieux) and damning with faint praise throughout, this
review's most revealing phrase is 'Fritz Lang seems to have lost some
of his old power ... '. Underlying this judgment is British film culture's
massive preference for European Lang (*The Testament of Dr Mabuse*,
Metropolis, *M*) over American Lang (*Western Union*, *Woman in the
Window*, *Scarlet Street*), a prejudice revelatory at bottom of an elitist
commitment to 'high art' and literary values over 'popular art' and
cinematic values. The review of *The Big Heat* in *Sight and Sound* is by
Lindsay Anderson and is more complex:

It seems a long time since Fritz Lang gave us a good film: in fact,
the sense of strain and stylistic pretentiousness in his recent work
– when it has not been mere commercial hokum – had almost
made one abandon hope. This makes it the more unfortunate that
his latest film should have passed almost unnoticed. For it is an
extremely good thriller, distinguished by precisely those virtues
which Lang's pictures have in the past few years so painfully
lacked: tautness and speed; modesty of intention; intelligent,
craftsmanlike writing. Above all, it is directed with a dramatic
incisiveness, a sharp-edged observation that keeps the pitch of
interest and excitement continuously high. ... *The Big Heat* is one
of those enjoyable films which make no great claims for
themselves, yet which so balance style and intention (like the
early Hitchcocks, for instance) that they are finally more
satisfying than many more ambitious works. The film lacks the
density of a *Maltese Falcon*; one or two of its elements are over-

> conventional. All the same, it creates its world, and proves that, when his interest is engaged, this director still has at his control the technique of a master.   (July–September 1954)

Lindsay Anderson (especially when engaging with a director he admires, like John Ford) is among the most sensitive of film critics. It is clear that he responds deeply to *The Big Heat* and that he is much less constrained by traditional British attitudes to Hollywood. However, his review cannot altogether get beyond seeing *The Big Heat* as craftsmanlike as opposed to seeing it as a piece of art as philosophically penetrating and stylistically complex as any in the cinema. A contemporary review which does precisely this is François Truffaut's in *Cahiers du Cinéma* (January 1954).

The seriousness with which *Cahiers* and Truffaut take Lang and *The Big Heat* is indicated immediately by the length of the review, which extends over three pages, and by its title – 'Aimer Fritz Lang'. Beginning with what *auteurist* critics have consistently seen as the philosophical core of Lang's films – 'Moral solitude, Man struggling alone against a universe which is half-hostile, half-indifferent, that is Lang's favourite theme... ' – Truffaut proceeds to a classic *auteurist* insertion of *The Big Heat* into the Lang canon, making no distinction between the European and American films.

Among the strands feeding into the differences in British and French attitudes to *The Big Heat* are the historically distinct perceptions of the USA held by Britain and France, the former seeing the USA as unsophisticated and errant younger sibling, the latter seeing it as revolutionary forerunner; the different weighting of the visual arts in British and French culture, the former primarily oriented to literature and drama, the latter more open to visual imagery; and perhaps the more favourable view in France of American popular culture which flowed from certain French artistic (e.g. Surrealism) and philosophical (e.g. Existentialism) movements.

The Big Heat was re-released in Britain in 1988, by which time it had undergone reconstruction within two quite separate discourses. Although its violence had been remarked upon in the 1950s and institutionally recognised by its 'X' Certificate, what could not have been foreseen was that one specific act of violence from the film would take on a momentum of its own in popular culture so that *The Big Heat* came to be remembered, often by people not particularly interested in cinema, as the film in which Lee Marvin throws boiling coffee in Gloria Grahame's face. That this perception took a deep hold on popular consciousness is indicated not only by Spanish director Pedro Almodóvar's spoof coffee commercial which recapitulates the act, but by the extent to which the reviews of the film on its 1988 re-release in Britain, in both the quality and the popular press, make reference to it. *The Times*, the *Financial Times*, the London *Evening Standard*, the *Daily Telegraph* and the *Independent* all refer to the scalding, which indicates how it had become something of a popular cultural intertext.

However, what is most striking about the 1988 British press response to *The Big Heat*, compared with that of 1954, is its *extent* and the quite different status now accorded the film in British (film) culture. Nothing could be further from the offhand dismissal or the grudging or qualified praise of the 1950s than, for example, the respectful and insightful piece by Judith Williamson in the *New Statesman*. Two quotations from this piece will indicate not only how far but in what directions British (film) culture had travelled since 1954:

> Grahame is the gangster's moll, while Ford figures as husband and father in an excessively idyllic family whose domestic scenes are, as in *Fatal Attraction*, disrupted first by the phone and then by physical violence. However, it is not an Other woman who is the source of evil here, but the mob or, more precisely, the fear and cowardice that allow it to operate.

and

> ... it is impossible to talk about [films'] sexual meanings without also looking at their construction ...

The specific discourses informing the above quotations are *feminism* and *textuality*, themselves part of the wider transformation of British social and intellectual life which has occurred, increasingly from the late 1960s, since the 1954 release of *The Big Heat*. Within this transformation the hegemony of (largely) literary film critics and reviewers has been challenged to the extent that sneering at (or grudgingly conceding the quality of) Hollywood films and other popular artefacts is no longer automatic.

What is most striking about Judith Williamson's review of *The Big Heat*, compared with the 1954 reviews, is the relaxed confidence (one is tempted to say 'naturalness') with which she engages in serious discussion of the film, a confidence born of the knowledge that she is addressing a substantial readership which does not find it at all odd to see Hollywood films discussed in this way. Like all cultural transformations, the route from seeing *The Big Heat* as merely 'craftsmanlike' to seeing it as the site of cultural tensions and formal richness is a complex and meandering one. However, some of the signposts are the publishing of books such as Richard Hoggart's *The Uses of Literacy* and Raymond Williams's *Culture and Society* and *The Long Revolution* in the 1950s and the 1960s; books which were taken up by a generation of intellectuals and teachers (many of them working-class beneficiaries of the 1944 Education Act) and refracted into a concern with the 'mass media' and a wish to validate the popular cultural choices of the class from which they came (Stuart Hall and Paddy Whannel's *The Popular Arts* is a key text here); second, the substantial influence of French film theory among younger critics in Britain, followed later by a heavy dose of general theory in the form of structuralism, semiotics, marxism, Saussurean linguistics and Lacanian psychoanalysis, disciplines then applied to film and imbricated with diverse feminisms from Europe and the United States; and, not least, the fact that these positions achieved influential institutional bases in, for example, the Centre for Contemporary Cultural Studies at the University of Birmingham, certain departments of the British Film Institute, the journal of film theory, *Screen*, and important sectors of British higher education, most notably the polytechnics.

If all this seems a long way from *The Big Heat* as text, the film itself was one of the sites over which these insurgent movements contested the hegemony of traditional British critical categories and values, and certain of these movements provided the most useful critical tools with which to discuss the film.

4

....
'THE BIG HEAT' AND CRITICAL METHOD –
A PERSONAL MEMOIR

In the late 1960s I started writing a book which was published in 1972 as *Underworld USA*. It offered a theoretical framework for understanding the form and development of the Hollywood crime movie and an account of several *auteurs*, including Fritz Lang, who had produced significant work within the genre. The chapter on Lang contained a detailed discussion of *The Big Heat*.

It would have been possible to write the present book purely from the point of view of the 1990s and to offer an analysis of *The Big Heat* in terms of how I now see it, with no necessary reference to *Underworld USA*. In some respects this would have been an easier option, but it would be evasive not to try to engage with the substantial criticisms which have been levelled at the earlier book. However, going back into the past to address the critiques of *Underworld USA* would be like opening a Pandora's Box. The way one writes about the cinema is never simply a matter of the critical orientation and vocabulary one chooses, never solely a matter of cinema *per se*. It goes much deeper than that, with implications for film pedagogy, for the policy and practice of the institutions within and through which cinema is discussed and, indeed, for the wider question of the relationship between cultural work and politics.

The preceding chapter offered a bare outline of several of the factors leading to the markedly more favourable reception of *The Big Heat* in British (film) culture in 1988 as opposed to the scant attention paid it in 1954. These factors together constituted a massive, continuing struggle about the terms in which cinema (indeed all art, 'popular' or 'high' – if these terms still retain any oppositional force) should be discussed and the relationship of that discussion to other areas of social experience. I was – and in a less institutionally-based sense still am – part of that struggle.

Coming from a Glasgow working-class background and having left school at fifteen to pursue a craft apprenticeship, I had gone to Glasgow University in 1957 as a mature student and undergone a relatively orthodox British training in, mainly, English Literature.

While not being as Leavisite as would perhaps have been the case at an *English* university, it was nevertheless largely formalist, untheoretical and depoliticised in the sense that the relationship between one's life in the English Literature classroom and one's life in the world was simply not addressed (this last point being *very* un-Leavisite). Although responding to particular teachers (John Rillie, Edwin Morgan and John Bryce stand out), I derived more relevance and excitement from books which were not prescribed, such as the Hoggart and Williams texts referred to in the last chapter, and the handful of books on the cinema then to be found on library shelves. Looking at today's plethora of books on the cinema, it is salutary to recall that in the 1950s and 1960s the only film books likely to be encountered in libraries were Paul Rotha's *The Film Till Now*, Siegfried Kracauer's *From Caligari to Hitler*, Arthur Knight's *The Liveliest Art* and S. M. Eisenstein's *The Film Sense*.

Training as a secondary school teacher in Glasgow in 1961–2, I was confronted even more starkly by the gulf between my university literary training and the cultural experiences of the children I taught. It was about this time that I came across the British Film Institute's Summer School, run then as now by the BFI's Education Department. It was a revelation to find figures such as Paddy Whannel, Jim Kitses and Alan Lovell talking seriously not only about cinema but also about how best cinema might be discussed with secondary school pupils and day-release students. Hollywood was central (though not exclusive) to this point of view, and the strategy (unlike virtually all formal education at the time) was to validate rather than condemn students' choices and help them to discriminate among their cinema (and other popular cultural) experiences. Stuart Hall and Paddy Whannel's *The Popular Arts* (1964) came to be a key text for those young teachers like myself who were trying to build syllabuses out of these ideas. The point of this preamble is to underline that our commitment to Hollywood in the 1960s was personal, pedagogical and ultimately political; a deliberate contesting of the elitist values of orthodox Eng. Lit. and of the wider British culture.

By the time I myself joined the BFI Education Department in 1968 (to replace V.F. Perkins, who had moved out into a teaching post), the department's pedagogical/political commitment to Hollywood had been augmented by an awareness of French *auteurism* which had entered British culture primarily through the journals *Oxford Opinion* and *Movie* (V.F. Perkins being a central figure in both), and by a more general exploration of film theory coming primarily from Peter Wollen, who at that time had responsibility, in the BFI Education Department, for publications and relations with higher education. As well as the BFI Education Department's annual Summer School, the main training ground for my generation of film teachers was the courses the BFI Education Department ran in conjunction with the Extra-Mural Department of the University of London. It was at one such course, Alan Lovell and Peter Wollen's 'Myth and Genre in the American Cinema' (in, I think, 1966–7), that *Underworld USA* began to form in my mind. Strongly marked by French *auteurism*, the book nevertheless tried to 'correct' the a-social dimension of *auteurism* by posing genre as a category within which questions of industry, text and audience could be addressed, although the overwhelming focus is on the second of these. *Underworld USA* (along with Jim Kitses' book on the Western, *Horizons West*) was to become quite influential in discussions of Hollywood and genre and, unsurprisingly given the milieu out of which it came, was readily adaptable into teaching programmes at every level of the educational system. This point about the need for one's theoretical system and critical practice to be pedagogically usable is important, and I will return to it.

But the history of our personal, pedagogical and political commitment to Hollywood cannot be discussed without reference to the politics of particular institutions. The BFI Education Department had become the intellectual centre of debate about the cinema in Britain, but the terms we used (*auteur*, genre, structuralism, semiology) antagonised the wider film culture to an extent that would hardly be credible now. The BFI itself mounted a governors' committee of inquiry into the activities of the department and in essence recommended that it stop being interested in ideas, that it be renamed the Educational Advisory Service, and that it simply service the expressed needs of teachers. Seven members of the department, including the Head, Paddy Whannel, and the Deputy Head, Alan Lovell, resigned. Over this same period *Screen*, the journal of the Society for Education in Film and Television (SEFT) – the main organisation of media studies teachers – transformed itself from a relatively eclectic and unadventurous media educational magazine into the leading journal of film theory in the English-speaking world, and began to embark upon the series of theoretical elaborations round Saussurean structuralism, Metzian semiology, Althusserian marxism and Lacanian psychoanalysis which were to characterise its work in the 1970s and 1980s.

The internal purge was a bitter experience for the members of the BFI Education Department, partly ameliorated, for those who remained, by the appointment of Douglas Lowndes as Head of the Educational Advisory Service. Lowndes, who had a substantial track record in the pedagogy of film-making (a 'practical' orientation which had commended itself to the same BFI management which had purged the Education Department's 'intellectuals'), was, like every thinking person in the post-1968 years, reassessing his own positions on (film) aesthetics and politics and their relationship, a process which left him much more theoretically informed and increasingly sympathetic to the work of the purged Education Department and of *Screen*. He and I analysed the events leading up to the purge and concluded that the key element which had allowed it to occur was the ghettoised position of the Education Department within the BFI and, in particular, its lack of support on the BFI Executive, at that time the BFI's top policy-making and executing committee, made up of the heads of departments and the directorate. The main result of the strategy we adopted on the basis of this analysis was my appointment as Head of Film Availability Services in 1974, after which the intellectual positions traditionally associated with the Education Department began to take root at a senior level in other BFI departments. In retrospect, the decade from 1974 seems dominated by the grind of administration, with Lowndes and I attempting to gain purchase on every Institute mechanism (appointments committees, for example) through which the balance of cultural attitudes might be altered so that an event like the purge of the Education Department could never occur again.

Through our membership of the BFI Executive we were able to initiate fundamental discussion of Institute policy, trying to replace the intuition- and taste-based practice – within which no justifications were made as to which films were acquired, preserved, screened or written about – with a debate-based policy which was open to public scrutiny.

The content of this policy, which came to be known as the 'key debates', was to be those questions which had preoccupied critics and theorists since the birth of cinema: authorship, genre, realism vs anti-realism, the relationship between films and the societies out of which they come, and so on. We also argued that heads of BFI departments should stop behaving like Chinese warlords and start subscribing to a common set of policy aims: when a topic was agreed to be important all BFI departments should gear their work round it simultaneously so that, for example, a major season be mounted at the National Film Theatre, new viewing copies struck by the National Film Archive, the BFI produce books and magazines on the topic, and so on.

I have reached an age when questions about the meaningfulness of my life seem more urgent. In professional (as in personal) terms there are regrets: a tendency to ride policy horses too hard and too fast; a disposition to advance policy through 'contestation' rather than alliance; and a failure to recognise the importance of emergent technologies. On good days I clutch at straws. One such is that our attempt to 'colonise' other sectors of the BFI with ideas traditionally associated with the Education Department has made it more difficult for people ignorant of or hostile to these ideas to be appointed to senior posts in the BFI, a practice common if not actually encouraged before 1974. The rising calibre of senior appointments in the BFI has, however, frequently been compromised by the BFI's encounter with Thatcherite ideas. I clutch at another straw when reading a review like Judith Williamson's of *The Big Heat* (discussed in Chapter 3). As a tiny part of the more general transformation in British culture, our writings, course structures and policy initiatives in the BFI helped create the situation in which a young critic can write respectfully and informedly about Hollywood cinema and know that there is a substantial constituency sharing these views.

I remained in the BFI until 1984 in charge of a large department with responsibility for the acquisition of films for the distribution library and film programming in regional film theatres and, from 1979, grant-giving to regional arts associations and other BFI-assisted bodies. From 1979, therefore, my department had direct purchase on the funding of the Society for Education in Film and Television and, with it, its journal *Screen*. As *Screen* developed its critique of orthodox British film culture and proposed alternatives, much of the vilification formerly directed exclusively at the BFI's Education Department now came to be aimed at *Screen* as well, with individual BFI heads of departments, governors and even, on occasion, senior figures in the Office of Arts and Libraries (the government department which funded the BFI) repeatedly raising the question why the BFI was funding a journal which was not only marxist but 'unreadable' as well. It fell to myself and the few senior BFI officers actively sympathetic to *Screen* (e.g. Douglas Lowndes, and Peter Sainsbury, Head of Production) to defend the journal, a cause to which Anthony Smith became converted after his appointment as Director of the BFI in 1978. However, the pressure against SEFT and *Screen* became harsher and more highly placed as Thatcherism took hold after 1979. I recall being with Anthony Smith when he received a letter from the senior civil servant at the Office of Arts and Libraries. The letter began, 'It has been brought to the Minister's [at that time Rhodes Boyson] attention that a particular school of thought is dominant in the Society for Education in Film and Television and its journal *Screen* ...' To his undying credit, Anthony Smith immediately drafted an articulate and passionate defence of liberal pluralist values, in particular intellectual freedom, which silenced the guns at the OAL for some time, although individuals in British film culture regularly complained to the Minister about what they saw as the 'marxist' bias of *Screen* and – ludicrously for anyone who has actually worked there – the BFI.

The obverse of defending SEFT and *Screen* within the BFI was that one's public criticisms of them had to be very muted, for there were people both inside and outside the BFI ready to use *any* criticism to malign the society and its journal. Clearly I regarded myself as an ally of *Screen*, and my own *Television and History* (1978) was greatly influenced by the Althusserianism which *Screen* had done so much to promote in the English-speaking world. However, I was becoming uneasy about the increasingly *abstract* nature of *Screen*'s theorising, particularly its adoption of Lacanian psychoanalysis as the key to film narrative and subject positioning, and the inevitability that implied of removing theoretical categories further away from conscious experience and therefore from widespread pedagogical and political use. Partly for the institutional reasons outlined above but also partly out of general support for *Screen*'s position, I remained publicly silent about this unease. However, in 1975 Alan Lovell, at the time editing the Film Culture section of the journal, invited me to contribute a brief piece on the television series *Days of Hope*. Thinking about the piece, and the extent to which *Screen* was indifferent to *Days of Hope* and was indeed ready to dismiss it for what seemed to me the most abstract of theoretical reasons, I concluded there was no way I could write about the series without taking *Screen* to task for its readiness to ignore six hours of peak-time television drama about the history of working-class struggles, a position it had been led into, it seemed to me, through its increasingly abstract theorising.

This view was shared by many in the film education community and surfaced within *Screen* itself at about the same time as my piece on *Days of Hope*. Indeed, the same issue (vol. 16, no. 4, Winter 1975–6) contained a piece, 'Psychoanalysis and Film', by several members of the editorial board which raised some of the same intellectual, pedagogical and political questions. These questions proved unresolvable within the editorial board, and in the issue of Summer 1976 (vol. 17, no. 2) the writers of the above piece, Ed Buscombe, Christine Gledhill, Alan Lovell and Christopher Williams, announced their resignation from the board in a statement which spelt out their reasons. The problem remained, however, that no serious alternative to *Screen* showed any sign of appearing, and the rearguard actions over policy, fought out within SEFT, had the effect of log-jamming *Screen*'s project without posing any real alternative. I found myself in the paradoxical position, as head of the BFI division which funded SEFT and *Screen*, of siding with *Screen* against its critics while sharing many of the latter's criticisms. The convention in arts funding is to avoid public schism at all costs and to manage policy change by way of informal discussion. Such was the case in the BFI's relationship with SEFT and *Screen*.

Inevitably, the two dimensions of *Underworld USA*, its *auteurism* and its theory of genre, were critiqued from the *Screen* perspective in, respectively, Steve Jenkins (ed), *Fritz Lang: The Image and the Look* (1981), and Steve Neale, *Genre* (1980). Jenkins locates *Underworld USA*'s account of Fritz Lang within classic French *auteurism* and its adaptation by American critics such as Andrew Sarris and Peter Bogdanovich, then offers his critique:

While writings of this kind have a polemical value in that they paid some serious attention to the latter half of the Lang-text [i.e. Lang's American films], ultimately they came to a dead-end as regards anything other than descriptions of the person Lang's world-view, as manifested thematically and stylistically through a body of work. The text becomes only a coherent, well-ordered signifier of despair. In order to move beyond this idea it is perhaps the very notion of coherence itself which needs to be deconstructed and historically located. Raymond Bellour, in his essay 'On Fritz Lang', writes: 'Lang plays a highly perverse game. It is through the lacunae, the lack he establishes, that he seems intelligible.' Yet it is noticeable that those writers previously cited who have attempted to deal positively with the Lang-text have done so by sealing over, for example, what might be regarded as the primary fissure within that text, i.e. the gap between the German and American work.

Jenkins's own commitment to the *Screen* perspective is apparent in his introduction to his own essay in *Fritz Lang: The Image and the Look*, 'Lang: Fear and Desire':

It is arguable that the most significant developments within film theory during the last ten years or so, certainly in the area of classical narrative cinema, have occurred around ideas involving the representation of women. This phrase covers a variety of approaches which have produced important advances in the study of, for example, stereotyping, genre, psychoanalysis and cinema, and so on. As a result, it would now be unjustifiable to produce a book of this kind which was not inflected by these general developments in film theory. The aim here is to account for the stylistic aspects of the Lang-text generally, and to describe a part of it in some detail in terms other than those which have previously dominated writing on Lang. This previous approach can be summed up in a sentence: 'The Lang-text represents various manifestations of the person Lang's fatalistic world-view.' This idea of fate in Lang can perhaps be most usefully displaced by constructing a reading which inserts – forcefully –

the question of the significance of the female presence within the Lang-text.

Such a critical project flows directly from the centrality in *Screen* of Lacanian psychoanalysis and its placing of sexual difference at the centre of the universe.

Taking a considered view of the *Screen* position is not easy, particularly as it relates to the critiquing of one's own work. However, there are several aspects of the *Screen* perspective, and Jenkins's deployment of it on *Underworld USA*, that I would now wish to concede. *Underworld USA*'s *auteurist* account of Lang is too neat and hermetically sealed. Like most *auteur* studies, its principal lack is solid, empirical, historical work on the context of production of each of Lang's films. Also, the besetting sin of early *auteurism*, it has a totalising, organicising thrust which seeks to explain every aspect of every film in terms of Lang's vision, despite the other, genre half of *Underworld USA* which proposed a quite different axis of understanding. Such an organicising urge fails to take account of the possibility opened up not only by *Screen* but also by French structuralist literary theory as influenced by marxism and pre-Lacanian psychoanalysis, of gaps, fissures and repressions in a text. Such a possibility is indeed signalled in Jenkins's remarks above, but the possibility is realisable in terms other than a totalising sexual difference. My own later analysis of *Floodtide* in *Scotch Reels: Scotland in Cinema and Television* (1982) deploys precisely this critical insight, but in relation to *class* rather than gender. Steve Jenkins and I would probably agree, however, that the most useful critical insight French literary and film theory has bequeathed us is that absence may be as textually significant as presence.

As I have indicated above, an important consideration for me when writing film criticism had always been the pedagogical and ultimately the political usefulness of the exercise. It is reasonable to apply the same criteria to Steve Jenkins's critique of *Underworld USA* and his reconstruction of Lang. Its most obvious political implication, as with Lacanian analysis generally, is for feminist (cultural) politics. That Jenkins's reconstruction has not been mobilised, to my knowledge, in these terms may be due in part to the pedagogical difficulty of rendering usable a category, the construction of sexual difference, which, in the

Lacanian discourse, occurs at a pre-conscious if not *unconscious* stage of human development. This is not to say that *all* Lacanian analysis is pedagogically useless. *Screen*'s translation of *Cahiers du Cinéma*'s analysis of Ford's *Young Mr Lincoln* has great pedagogic usefulness, but that analysis locates the film in a number of discourses – e.g. history, technology, genre, author – as well as psychoanalysis.

There is another aspect of Jenkins's critique and reconstruction which smacks of, if not bad faith, then of having one's cake and eating it. The essay makes great play of rejecting the notion of Fritz Lang as '*auteur*' and referring to any Lang film (and indeed the entire Lang corpus) as a/the Lang-text. While, at one level, it is possible to be sympathetic to this strategy as a way of signalling the over-determination of any film by a number of different systems (studio, genre, contemporary technology, etc.) and as a polemic against the Romantic notion of the director as 'onlie begetter', it is worth noting that such analyses continue to be constructed under the sign of the *auteur* – as, for example, in the title of Jenkins's book. Also, the proof of the critical pudding is in the eating. Consider the following passage:

> A link between the 'freezing' of characters as elements of decor and the concentration on significant objects is the further tendency within the Lang-text to isolate in close-up parts of the human body. Clearly this is not unique to Lang, but it *is* a noticeable stylistic feature.... Examples abound: Masimoto's hand, upon which drops of rain are falling . . . in *Spione*; the hand marked with the letter M . . . in *M*; the shot of Hofmeister's foot at the beginning of *Testament of Dr Mabuse*; eyes peering through the rear window of the robbery car in *You Only Live Once*; Helen and Joe's hands meeting on the escalator rail in *You and Me*; a finger on the trigger in *Manhunt*; . . . crossed fingers in *Scarlet Street* . . .

Auteurism must change in order to remain as it is!

The act of criticism, particularly when one erects new theoretical definitions of a field, is akin to painting oneself into a corner. It is quite difficult to think oneself out of the critical/theoretical system one has erected. One is therefore dependent on other critics pointing out the limitations of and contradictions within one's own position. This was precisely what Steve Neale's *Genre* did for the author of *Underworld USA*. Like Steve Jenkins's book, *Genre* drew attention to the traditional Romantic conception of the artist which informed the book, both in its chapters on individual directors and in its formulations regarding the relationship between directors and genres. More specifically, Neale demonstrates the limitations of the deployment of iconography – central to *Underworld USA* – as a way of dealing with the entire visual field of cinema, and critiques the book's tendency to misconstrue the relationship between the 'reality' of American society and its representation in the gangster film/thriller. Quite apart from its valuable critique of *Underworld USA* and other critical writings on genre, Neale's book throws useful emphasis on those genres (e.g. the horror movie, the musical, the melodrama) less obviously connected than are the gangster film/thriller and the Western to particular moments in American history, and on the relationship of particular genres to dominant forms of narrative and to the 'institution cinema' – the entire apparatus for the regular delivery of pleasurable stories through a variety of mechanisms. However, *Genre* is vitiated by the same problem which afflicts *Fritz Lang: The Image and the Look* – its deployment of Lacanian psychoanalysis and its urge to explain the functioning of particular genres in terms of differing modalities of gendered subjectivity.

I have suggested that the acid test for any theoretical position is its capacity to produce workable categories which can be incorporated into teaching schemata. The author himself being a teacher, *Genre* is exemplary in the attention it gives to the pedagogy of genre (a whole appendix is given over to its discussion). It is surely significant, however, that the topics foregrounded in the appendix are the very traditional ones of genre recognition and differentiation and the narrative pattern of classic (Hollywood) cinema – equilibrium/ disruption/new equilibrium. There is no reference whatsoever in the pedagogy section to the Lacanian apparatus on which the book is predicated.

It is more than likely that the *Screen*-influenced writers who critiqued *Underworld USA*, and whom I in turn have critiqued, will nowadays share the anti-abstract position I am advancing. Such a shift is implicit in the changing marxist problematic we all inhabit, albeit with different emphases. There is, for example, in my own writings, a discernible shift from the tight Althusserianism of *Television and History* (1978) to the more relaxed theoretical framework of *Scotch Reels* (1982), which owes more to Antonio Gramsci, Michel Foucault and Edward Said. Also, the anti-totalising mood has been given theoretical utterance under the sign of post-modernism in the work of Baudrillard, Lyotard and others, and this has had an effect on critical practice. However, I would wish to make a distinction between a suspicion of *abstract* theorising, which I very much share, and the tendency of diverse post-modernisms to jettison what have been called 'grand narratives', holistic explanations of history and social life. While taking on board much that has been written under the rubric of post-modernism, I am certainly unwilling to abandon the search for theoretical explanations of the way things are, particularly explanations which seek to clarify the relationship between economic and political power on the one hand and discursive systems on the other.

There is one further critical method which should be mentioned, a method which unusually has come out of the practice of the Hollywood industry itself. The last few years have seen the publication of several DIY books on screenwriting, including Syd Field's *Screenplay* (1982) and *The Screenwriter's Workbook* (1984) and Michael Hauge's *Writing Screenplays That Sell* (1988). Even more publicly visible have been the regular 'story structure' courses run by Robert McKee which attract aspiring and practising screenwriters, producers, agents and diverse personnel in and around the film industry. McKee describes the contents of his course as a systematised version of craft knowledge which has been around in Hollywood for decades.

Ironically, the critical category which this nuts-and-bolts account of how to write a classic two-hour Hollywood screenplay has most in common with is that highly abstract *Screen* invention, the 'classic realist text', with its characteristic equilibrium/disruption/new equilibrium structure and its 'hierarchy of discourses'. You would look in vain, however, for any further resemblance to the *Screen* position. There are no gaps, fissures and repressions here unless wilfully created by the screenwriter, as implied in the McKee axiom, 'If a scene is about what a scene is about, you're in trouble' – a pithy rendering of the critical point that a scene works better when there is a level of meaning which is not up-front in the words spoken by the characters. What McKees's and other DIY screenwriting programmes offer is a format: one hundred and twenty pages, one page equal to one minute of screen time, a turning point (i.e. an incident which spins the story off into a new direction) on or about page 30 and another on or about page 90, fourteen different kinds of plot, ways of developing characters and sub-plots, and so on. The method (attended though it often is by ignorance or derision of other kinds of cinema) offers an unrivalled insight into how classic Hollywood movies are constructed.

I am prepared to be eclectic in my discussion of *The Big Heat*, drawing where appropriate on film history, *auteurism*, genre study, structuralism, post-structuralism and McKee-type DIY discourse on screenwriting. The detailed analysis of *The Big Heat* which follows is more in the way of an affectionate settling of accounts with a film which I have admired for nearly forty years. That it revolves primarily round questions of *mise-en-scène* and narrative structure is a fair indication of one important area of my current concerns. One of the regrettable effects of the *Screen* hegemony was that the *Movie* critics, always the best on the British scene in their awareness of *mise-en-scène*, tended to lapse into silence. I have often felt that the rise of *Screen* and the decline of *Movie* contributed to the situation, which I encountered repeatedly as teacher and external examiner, in which students made confident judgments about the ideological implications of particular texts while displaying quite a feeble grasp of textual processes. One of the outcomes of recent changes in the curriculum is the emergence of many practically-oriented moving images courses. With the proviso that the most important questions to be asked of films are, in the last analysis, questions of ideology, I hope the following *mise-en-scène*-based discussion of *The Big Heat* will be helpful to this new generation of students. After all, one's criticism should be pedagogically and politically useful.

5

....

'THE BIG HEAT' AS COMPLEX TEXT

It has often been remarked that the opening shot of *The Big Heat* is among the starkest in the cinema and (in terms of what is to follow) the most appropriate. A police .38 in big close-up lies on a desk. A hand reaches into frame and takes the gun out of frame. The sound of a single shot is heard and a body, gun in hand, slumps across the desk. It is a most appropriate 'overture' for this most violent (of its time) of films, but it is also the most perfect of generic images to introduce a gangster film.

Classic *auteurism* would tend to put this choice of opening image down simply to Fritz Lang's creativity, and there is a sense in which this holds water. After all, Lang supervised the shooting of the image and its insertion into the key point of the film's opening. However, scrutiny of Lang's papers in the Cinémathèque Française reveals a more complex process at work. Sydney Boehm's original scenario shows the figure (named Deery in Boehm's script, as in the novel, but Duncan in the film) committing suicide in full view with the gun pressed to his temple. The reason for the change in the manner of shooting is conveyed in a memo, dated 10 April 1953, to Fritz Lang from Robert Arthur, the film's producer, indicating that he has had discussions with the censorship authorities regarding the suicide scene and that if the scene were to be shot as written it would infringe the censorship code. Arthur's memo then goes on to propose that the scene be shot very much as it appears in the finished film. Leblanc and Devismes devote a section of their book to discussion of this, a section headed – provocatively for purist *auteurists* – 'Quand le Producteur met en scène' ('When the Producer directs').

The remainder of the opening scene, and the three scenes which follow it, have rightly been hailed as a masterly condensation of film narrative. Following Duncan's suicide, his wife Bertha appears, examines the contents of the suicide letter he has addressed to the District Attorney, picks up the telephone and proceeds to dial. Mike Lagana (Alexander Scourby) – crime boss of the city, as it will emerge – is seen being wakened by one of his men to take Bertha Duncan's call. He compliments her for calling him rather than the District Attorney, then he makes a telephone call himself. The call is answered by Debby Marsh (Gloria Grahame), who asks Vince Stone (Lee Marvin) to take it. The next scene opens with the flash of a police photographer's camera taking pictures of the suicide scene. This is the scene in which Sergeant Dave Bannion (Glenn Ford) is introduced. Bannion, the central figure in the film, is rumpled and tieless, summoned from his bed to investigate a cop's suicide. Bannion's harassed, honest poverty will be counterpointed throughout the film with the corrupt luxury of Lagana, Stone and their associates.

In just a few minutes of screen time all the film's major protagonists – with the exception of Bannion's wife Katie (Jocelyn Brando) – are introduced. In addition, because of the audience's capacity to make genre recognitions, stemming from familiarity with the gangster film, an enormous amount of information is conveyed simultaneously through dress, decor and the disposition of figures in relation to each other. Lagana, for instance, is seen wearing silk pyjamas in an enormous, luxurious bed. He is attended, acolyte-like, by George, a muscular young man in a white dressing gown.

Lying behind Lagana's representation is a tradition of representing crime bosses as languidly luxurious which goes back to the classic gangster movies of the 1930s and 1940s (e.g. Edward G. Robinson in *Key Largo*). Critics have also detected, in the manner of George's representation, homosexual overtones in the scene. Some years after *Underworld USA* appeared, when the gay movement was becoming more politically active, I was taken to task by a gay friend for not distancing myself from the book's argument that unpleasant characters in the gangster film/thriller were often presented in terms of what I had called 'aberrant sexuality'. I promised my friend that if ever *Underworld USA* were reprinted I would make sure this was corrected. Since the book was not reprinted, I am happy at this point to revise the argument to the effect that mainstream cinema, being ideologically close to the contours of the dominant value system, often attributes sexual traits which it perceives as aberrant to unsympathetic characters in certain genres, most notably the gangster film/thriller and the *film noir*. Such, certain critics have suggested, is the case – though very subtly conveyed through dress, action, lighting and decor – in the Lagana/George bedroom scene.

'A masterly condensation of film narrative': Mrs Duncan telephones

Lagana is wakened to take her call

Debby answers Lagana

Vince takes his call

The police photographer

Bannion's 'harassed, honest poverty'

The intended homosexual overtones of the scene are perhaps more explicit in Boehm's scenario, which contains a scene, not included in the film, in which George is introduced. It reads:

> He has the look of a thirty-year old footballer. ... He is naked from the waist up and lies on the bed cover. ... Nearby is a small statuette of a modern style Atlas. It is engraved 'George Rose – Champion Weightlifter 1948 – Heavyweight Division'.

Athleticism, particularly relating to Classical Greek models, was a coded way of signalling homosexuality in the cinema at this time.

The introduction of Debby Marsh is also replete with generic meaning, as with Lagana conveyed in dress, decor, and body language and, in Debby's case, hair colour and make-up. With her high-lighted hair, heavy make-up, shiny dress and lolling posture, Debby is the classic gangster's moll, another tradition of cinematic representation going back to the 1930s gangster movie (e.g. Jean Harlow in *The Public Enemy*). When Debby passes the telephone to Vince to take Lagana's call, she pauses on her way to another room to admire her reflection in a mirror, a feature which has been remarked upon by *auteurist* critics in terms of Lang's German inheritance and his fondness for expressionist reduplication of images. This point too has a sustainable element in it, by reference to Lang's other films and also to a later scene in which Bannion first interviews Bertha Duncan, but the purist *auteurist* position is again rendered more complex by reference to Lang's papers. They contain a letter, dated 27 February 1953, from Jerry Wald, Executive Producer of *The Big Heat*, to Robert Arthur, Sydney Boehm and Fritz Lang, which reads:

> You should underline the extent to which Debby is anxious to preserve her beauty and the extent her face is important to her before the incident with the coffee. If you make her beauty the principal object of her vanity, the burning of her face becomes that much more tragic for her.

Debby is repeatedly seen admiring herself in mirrors, a motif as readily attributable to Wald's intervention as to Lang's vision.

There is a formal device that elegantly links the scenes in which the main protagonists are introduced, a formal device drawn from the generic armature of the gangster film. Technology is central to the genre: weapons, telephones, cars, etc. It is precisely the linking motif of this generic technology which holds the opening sequence of *The Big Heat* together, most obviously in the telephone linking Bertha Duncan/ George/Lagana/Debby/Vince; but it is another aspect of generic technology, the flash of a police photographer's camera over Duncan's body, which opens the scene introducing Bannion. It is in the scene following this that Bannion has his first interview with Bertha Duncan. The scene is essentially about lying, Bertha Duncan pretending to be the grieving widow and inventing a story about her husband's ill-health to explain his suicide. One of the reasons Lang is admired as a film-maker is the extent to which in his work the *real* meaning of a scene is often conveyed by specifically cinematic means, by the *mise-en-scène*. Before Bannion enters the room Bertha Duncan is seen rehearsing the role of grieving widow in front of a mirror, and mirror images play an important role in the scene.

Mrs Duncan rehearses her role

Unlike the thriller or *film noir*, in which the audience is often as much in the dark as the central investigative figure and the narrative drive consists in both investigator and audience finding things out simultaneously, in *The Big Heat* the audience is in possession of substantially more information than Dave Bannion, for example about the complicity of Tom and then Bertha Duncan with the mob. Part of the pleasure for the audience, therefore, is watching Bannion put the pieces of the jigsaw together, watching him change from viewing Duncan's death as a simple suicide to seeing it as an act with much more sinister ramifications. Another set of pleasures is at work charting the change in Bannion from law-abiding cop to the very edge of becoming a thug like Vince Stone.

These and other developments can be approached by a number of critical methods. Syd Field, one of the more prominent teachers of the mechanics of (classical Hollywood) screenwriting, suggests that the following structure is broadly applicable to any classical Hollywood screenplay:

Act 1	Act 2		Act 3
setup	*confrontation*		*resolution*
	plot point 1		plot point 2
	pp. 25–27		pp. 85–90

Field defines a plot point as 'an incident or event that "hooks" into the action and spins it around into another direction'. Within this paradigm, Duncan's suicide and Bannion's initial investigation into it are the 'setup'; the plot point 1 (which, according to Field, normally occurs between pages 25 and 27 of the script, is the killing of Katie Bannion which 'spins [the action] around into another direction' by transforming Bannion from investigator into avenger; the 'confrontation' is Bannion taking on the mob virtually single-handed; the plot point 2 is Debby's switching of allegiances from Vince to Bannion or perhaps Debby's killing of Bertha Duncan, which precipitates the disclosure of Tom Duncan's suicide letter and the 'resolution' of the film.

Structuralism as a critical method has had considerable success with popular American films because of the extent to which they are constructed around polar opposites. Thus *The Big Heat* could be laid out as a grid as follows:

Bannion (and Katie)	Lagana/Stone/Debby
honesty	corruption
simplicity	luxury
marriage	sexual liaison
home	house/apartment
parenthood	sterility
sharing	selfishness
democracy	hierarchy
tenderness	brutality
light	dark

This grid, by no means exhaustive, is clearly articulated in *The Big Heat*, but where it becomes more interesting than other gangster movies which might deploy similar sets of oppositions is in the extent to which certain of the protagonists shift categories and move towards becoming their polar opposites. This is particularly true of Bannion, after his wife's death, and Debby.

The first domestic scene between Bannion and Katie is strategically placed after the darkness and corruption of the Duncan and Lagana milieux and the brashness of Vince Stone's penthouse. Doubtless feminist critics nowadays would take a cooler look at *The Big Heat*'s construction of Bannion's 'domestic bliss', but within the ideology of the film it is meant to function in opposition to the world of the Duncans, Lagana, Debby and Vince. Unlike these milieux, the Bannion home is suffused with light. The art historian Erwin Panofsky has written about checkered tablecloths signifying a poor but respectable milieu in early American cinema. *The Big Heat* does not quite offer this, but it does present Katie in a checkered pinafore, constructing her as, in the words of Leblanc and Devismes, 'la femme idéale américaine'. Within the overall patriarchal ideology that suffuses the Dave/Katie relationship, there is a conscious attempt to suggest a warmer and more egalitarian relationship than the Tom Duncan/Bertha Duncan, Lagana/George, Vince/Debby relationships previously seen or implied. Bannion helps lay the table as Katie sets out the food; she takes a sip from his drink and draws on his cigarette. Also the mood of the scene is considerably lighter than what has gone before, with the Bannions' relationship being presented in terms of friendly banter. The banter is interrupted by a telephone call from one of Bannion's colleagues with the news that a woman has contacted the police department suggesting that Duncan could not possibly have killed himself. The scene ends with the camera moving in to the notepad on which Bannion has written 'Lucy Chapman. The Retreat'.

The Big Heat is a beautifully paced film. To use the terminology of Syd Field and Robert McKee, the first act, up to the killing of Katie Bannion, could be tracked in terms of the escalating intrusion of the ugly world of Lagana and Stone into the 'bliss' of the Bannion home. The first intrusive telephone call which ends the scene described above is apparently innocuous, a simple message asking Bannion to contact Lucy Chapman. However, it is a message which sends him into the tacky and (as it will emerge) violent world of the downtown bar, 'The Retreat', and introduces him to the woman, Lucy Chapman, whose torture and killing will begin to crack Bannion's certainty that Duncan's death was a simple suicide. The second intrusion into the Bannion home racks the tension up a bit. It is an anonymous call from Larry Gordon (Adam Williams), which is both an obscene call to Katie and a warning to Bannion to back off from further investigation of Duncan's death. The intrusion into the Bannion home culminates in the car bomb which kills Katie.

Looked at again structurally, it can be seen that the bright, friendly world of the Bannion home counterpoints both the dark world of the Duncan and Lagana milieux (and the brash milieu of Vince Stone) on the one side and the bleak world of 'The Retreat' on the other. Lucy is, in her own words, 'a B-girl' at 'The Retreat', and her interview with Bannion yields the first piece of evidence that Duncan might have been 'on the take', the fact that he owned 'a summer place... down in Lakeside'. However, the scene is played so as to make Bannion hostile to Lucy and sceptical about her story that Duncan was about to divorce his wife and marry her. Making Bannion hostile to Lucy in this scene increases his bitterness and sense of guilt in a later scene in which he identifies Lucy's body in the county morgue. But before that scene he revisits Bertha Duncan and, still sympathetic to her, asks for details of when 'the summer place' was bought and how much it cost 'to have the material to offset any insinuations [Lucy] might make'. Bannion is surprised by Bertha Duncan's haughty refusal to divulge any details.

As mentioned in my reference to the earlier scene between Bannion and Bertha Duncan with regard to lying, mirrors and the reduplication of images, Lang is admired for the resonance of his *mise-en-scène*, for his deployment of the resources of cinema to provide information. There is a fine example of this in the scene of Bannion's second interview with Bertha Duncan. The scene ends with Bannion's departure, after he has failed to get the information he wanted about the lakeside house, but the *mise-en-scène* closes not on Bannion leaving but on Bertha Duncan looking out of her window. This image then begins to dissolve into another image, a teletype machine printing out a message which, when it is handed to Bannion, we see reads:

> ATTENTION HOMICIDE DIV … KENPORT POLICE. UNIDENTIFIED WOMAN FOUND DEAD 6.26 A.M. OFF COUNTY PARKWAY. THROWN FROM CAR AFTER BEATING AND TORTURE. DRESS AND SHOES LABELED LAKESIDE FASHION SHOP. DESCRIPTION … WFA … ABOUT 28, 118 LBS, 5 FT 5 INS. BROWN EYES AND HAIR. FAIR COMPLEXION. CONTACT DR T.S. KANE, HILLSIDE COUNTY MEDICAL EXAMINER

The cinematic dissolve is often used, as here, to indicate the passing of time between two scenes, but it is sometimes used to pose a relationship between them. This particular dissolve suggests, by purely cinematic means, the implication of Bertha Duncan in Lucy Chapman's death.

The specific resources of cinema, in this case lighting, are further used to highlight the teletype message's reference to the Lakeside fashion shop. Bearing in mind that the message is held in Bannion's hand and he, as well as the audience, is reading it, by highlighting the Lakeside part of the message, Lang is suggesting by cinematic means Bannion's perception that the unidentified woman is Lucy Chapman and the fact that he has not taken her story seriously. This is underlined by the next scene in which Bannion, having identified the body, is talking with the County Medical Examiner:

CME: … You saw those cigarette burns on her body?

BANNION (bitterly): Yes, I saw them. Every single one of them!
CME: What's that name again?
BANNION: Miss Chapman. Lucy Chapman.

In the scene which follows, Bannion is taken to task by his superior, Lieutenant Wilks (Willis Bouchey), for bothering Mrs Duncan. The general feeling, supported by dialogue elsewhere in the film, is that Wilks, while not actively corrupt, is going to do nothing to antagonise powerful figures like Lagana and is simply passing on the pressure from 'upstairs' to impede Bannion.

Leblanc and Devismes discuss this particular scene in great detail in relation to their overall argument that Lang produces a 'double scenario' in his 'rewriting' of Sydney Boehm's original screenplay. They refer to Boehm's original scenario, Lang's brief manuscript additions (e.g. 'Wilks washes his hands'), and the quite complexly mounted scene as realised in the film. Rightly, they note the Lady Macbeth-like associations of Wilks washing his hands (although Pontius Pilate might be a more pertinent reference here), then they consider why Wilks's movements – amounting to an encircling of Bannion, who is seated opposite Wilks's desk in the classic interview position – are so complex in this scene. Leblanc and Devismes' view is that the 'natural' way to have realised the scene would have been in a shot/reverse shot format, with Wilks seated in the dominant position behind the desk and Bannion seated opposite him. However, they argue, a shot/reverse shot implies both a clarity of exchange and (all other things being equal) an equality of characters. The complex prowling movements of Wilks are therefore, they suggest, more appropriate to the clouded moral terrain between the two men, where all is not revealed and the discourse changes from Wilks's 'request' that Bannion stop bothering Bertha Duncan to his ordering him to do so, the order, incidentally, delivered at the point when Wilks is seated behind his desk in his role as Bannion's superior.

Leblanc and Devismes' argument is an extremely complex and sophisticated one, whose validity individual viewers should test against their own experience of the scene. Whether or not it ultimately convinces is less important than its value as a critical method requiring careful attention to cinematic processes, in this case the movement of

Above: Lt Wilks: Pontius Pilate or Lady Macbeth?
Below: Dissolve from Wilks to 'The Retreat'

actors in relation to each other and to the camera. Leblanc and Devismes' account of this scene closes on a point not dissimilar to that made above regarding the dissolve from Bertha Duncan's face at the window to the teletype machine pounding out the news of Lucy Chapman's death. They note that the final shot of the scene is from behind Wilks's back (he is now seated at his desk) as Bannion disappears through the door. As Wilks exhales a cloud of cigarette smoke, the shot begins to dissolve to the next scene, at 'The Retreat', in the form of a close-up of a barman's hand holding up a glass to test its clarity and polish. Leblanc and Devismes see this transition from 'smokescreen' to clarity as a comment on Wilks's ambiguous position and Bannion's drive to get at the facts. Bannion enters 'The Retreat' to question the barman holding up the glass.

Following the intrusion of Larry Gordon's threatening phone call into the Bannion home, Bannion, casting all caution to the winds, goes straight to the top, to Lagana's palatial house. He comments bitterly to a policeman on guard there about Lagana's round-the-clock protection by the police department. In certain respects the scene of Bannion's visit to Lagana's house has the narrative function of filling out the brief glimpse we have had of Lagana in the opening sequence of the film. The obvious trappings of wealth, and the extensive police guard, confirm his status and his grip on the levers of political power, and there is a specific mechanism which further locates Lagana within the tradition of the gangster movie. Leading Bannion into his study, Lagana pauses by a portrait of an old lady above the fireplace:

> My mother – a great old lady. They broke the mold when they made her. She died last May. She lived here with me. Had her own suite of rooms – her own bath – everything. Never got over being surprised about my success ...

Lagana's Italian origin looks back to some of the earliest gangster movies of the 1930s, specifically to Tony Camonte in *Scarface* and Rico in *Little Caesar*, and forward to the Corleone family of *The Godfather*. Indeed, it is possible to think of Mike Lagana as Tony Camonte twenty years on, hoodlum turned 'respectable' businessman. This recalls Daniel Bell's description of crime in American society as 'a queer ladder of social mobility'. More specifically, the reference to Lagana's mother recalls the importance of mothers in the earliest gangster movies (often as the repository of old-world, communitarian values set against the new-world individuality of the gangsters themselves), especially in *The Public Enemy* and *Little Caesar*, a tradition reworked in explicitly Freudian terms shortly before *The Big Heat* was made in *White Heat* (1949), and later recapitulated in *Bloody Mama* (1969).

The careful pacing of *The Big Heat* has already been referred to. It is in Bannion's visit to Lagana's home that the film reveals, in its dialogue, Bannion's capacity for bitterness and violence:

> LAGANA: I've seen some dummies in my time, but you're in a class by yourself.
> BANNION: I'm stupid because I want some answers about a murder, is that it?
> LAGANA: Shut up and get out.
> BANNION: We don't talk about these things in this house, do we? No, it's too elegant. Nice kids – party – painting of

Mike Lagana and mother: icon of the gangster movie

Mama up there on the wall. No place for a stinking cop! It's only a place for a hoodlum who built this house out of twenty years of corruption and murder! I'm going to tell you something. You know, you couldn't plant enough flowers around here to kill the smell.

The violence in Bannion explodes more graphically when Lagana's man, George, attempts to eject him. Such a foreshadowing of Bannion's internal violence is dramatically necessary (to use the terminology of the DIY screenwriting method) since this scene abuts closely on the scene which will rob Bannion of his wife. The DIY screenwriting method is much preoccupied with dramatic weighting, with the idea that an emotion can be heightened by counterpointing it with a reverse emotion. As illustrated here in the scene where Katie Bannion is blown up by a car bomb meant for her husband, which contains the most intimate moments between them just before she goes outside to start the car.

As indicated, the killing of Katie is, to use the DIY screenwriting term, the 'plot point' which spins the story round in a new direction. Up to this point the audience's question 'What will happen next?' – the central question of all narrative – has related to Bannion as investigator into the circumstances of Tom Duncan's death. After Katie's death, Bannion's investigation is personal – 'Who killed my wife?' The audience's interest is still centred on an investigation, but it is joined by a new narrative trajectory: how far will Bannion go down the road to becoming like Vince Stone and Larry Gordon? The film from this point proceeds to strip away those elements which differentiate Bannion from the mobsters. There is a scene in which Bannion indicates to the corrupt Police Commissioner, Higgins, that he is aware of the latter being in Lagana's pocket. Higgins suspends him and demands Bannion's badge and gun. Bannion returns the badge but, significantly, retains the gun. Even more significantly, this scene is followed by Bannion standing alone in his now empty house. It will be recalled that the film's opening sequences created a specific opposition, achieved through lighting, decor and performance, between the milieus of the Duncans, Lagana and Stone on the one hand and the Bannions on the other. The closing up of the Bannion house (Joyce, his daughter, has been sent to live with her aunt and uncle) is the poignant moment when Bannion is propelled into the twilight world of the mob, virtually indistinguishable in his actions from those he hunts.

Part of the skill in constructing a screenplay is knowing at what point to reveal information to produce the greatest dramatic effect. When Katie Bannion is killed, the audience *suspects* the involvement of Lagana and the mob in her death and, before that, in the death of Lucy Chapman. Indeed the *mise-en-scène* reveals the connection between the latter and Bertha Duncan. But their involvement is made explicit only in the scene following Bannion's desolation in his now empty house when Mike Lagana, visiting Stone's penthouse, takes Larry Gordon to task for bungling the disposal of Lucy Chapman's body and the attempted killing of Bannion. The revelation of the information at this precise point creates understanding of and, in dramatic if not moral terms, sympathy for Bannion's lust for vengeance.

But the scene of Lagana's visit to Vince Stone works on several other levels. Its choreography is exemplary in its handling of multiple characters: Debby, Vince, Larry, Lagana and George. It includes a reinforcement of Debby's love affair with her mirror image; it states perfectly, in its disposition of the actors, the hierarchical relationship between Lagana (seated) and Vince/Larry (standing), and effortlessly shifts the scene to new concerns by having Lagana and Vince move out to the balcony, Lagana framed with the lighted skyscrapers of the city around and beneath him. When Vince offers to handle the Bannion killing himself, Lagana says:

> Vince, you worry me. We've stirred up enough headlines. The election's too close. Things are changing in this country, Vince. A man who can't see that hasn't got eyes. Never get the people steamed up. They start doing things. Grand juries – election investigations – deportation proceedings. I don't want to land in the same ditch with the Lucky Lucianos.

The setting and the framing of this scene allows both the suggestion of Lagana's control of the city and the capacity of its anonymous citizens to get 'steamed up' to emerge simultaneously. Incidentally, the specific references in the above dialogue locate *The Big Heat* – as does the overall narrative – within that cycle of 1950s gangster movies (*Murder Inc*, *Inside the Mafia*, *The Brothers Rico*) which flowed from the smashing of a nationwide murder organisation by New York District Attorney Burton Turkus, and from the Kefauver Committee hearings into organised crime in 1951.

The scene closes with Lagana in frame talking about the capacity of 'the people' to organise and fight back against crime. It is not by accident that the following sequence produces precisely such an instance of a very ordinary citizen, the disabled Selma Parker, getting 'steamed up' and providing Bannion with the first hard lead in his investigation, the name 'Larry' and the fact that he can be contacted at 'The Retreat'. This sequence is also analysed in considerable depth (nineteen pages of comment, reproduced script materials and frame stills) by Leblanc and Devismes, their overall concern being how the original scenario of Sydney Boehm is reworked and transformed by Lang's revisions of the script and by his *mise-en-scène*. They reveal, for instance, how Lang transformed a foul-mouthed, disabled newsvendor called Selma, in the Boehm scenario, into the sympathetic figure of Selma Parker. The disability is retained, but Leblanc and Devismes suggest that the Boehm scenario uses a traditional Hollywood device whereby moral flaws are represented by physical defects. By contrast, the physical disability operating in Lang's *mise-en-scène* is suggestive of the imprisonment of a basically humane person working for an indifferent employer and, perhaps more generally, of a representative of the citizenry under Lagana. Certainly the sequence is replete with images of imprisonment, as will be seen.

The sequence shows Bannion's visit to a car graveyard to check out a list of mechanics who might have worked on the bomb which killed Katie. Milieu is an important dimension of *mise-en-scène*. This is much stressed by the manuals on screenwriting, which may speak of a milieu 'earning its place' in the screenplay. From this point of view, the car graveyard in *The Big Heat* evokes echoes of the manner of Katie's death. Unlike Boehm's original scenario, in which the owner of the car graveyard, Atkins, is friendly towards Bannion, in the film he is cool and evasive, provoking anger in Bannion and thereby allowing the scene to reinforce the suggestion already made of the barely repressed violence within him. It is Atkins's employee, Selma Parker, who, behind his back, gives Bannion the information he seeks. This part of the sequence takes place with Bannion and Selma Parker talking to each other through a wire-mesh fence, which creates the incarceratory imagery in which Selma is 'imprisoned'. But Bannion too is imprisoned by the dehumanising hatred and lust for revenge which consume him. We have seen him leave the police force and refuse help from former colleagues and the church. Although we have heard that his daughter is staying with an aunt and uncle, significantly we do not see Bannion with them, up to this point. To have shown Bannion in a family milieu would have softened and humanised him.

The ending of the scene between Bannion and Selma Parker and the dissolve which links it to the succeeding scene provide a classic example of cinematic *mise-en-scène*, marshalled as they are to complex and contradictory meanings. Towards the end of the exchange between Selma Parker and Bannion, the latter realises both that he has been given important information but also that Selma Parker has reached out to him in the depths of his despair. It is a tribute to Glenn Ford – performance being another dimension of *mise-en-scène* – that emotions

Bannion's entrapment

appropriate to both these factors register on his face. This is the moment at which Bannion begins his reintegration into the human race, but the dissolve here says something else as well. The final shot of the scene is of Bannion photographed through the wire-mesh fence. He is still imprisoned, cut off. The transition between shots tells us from what. The dissolve is from Bannion behind the wire fence to his child's pram and doll. The shot opens out to reveal the apartment of Bannion's in-laws. Bannion is with them. The *mise-en-scène* is therefore beginning to reintegrate Bannion with other human beings but at the same time withholding total reintegration. The Bannion character is still required dramatically to signify reservoirs of hatred in order to fulfil its role in the film.

As part of his reintegration, Bannion enlists the help of his brother-in-law to ring 'The Retreat' at an appointed time and ask for 'Larry'; Bannion will be there to identify the man called to the phone. The strategy fails, but the scene maintains in play two important elements in the film and initiates a third. Debby, Vince and his henchmen are in 'The Retreat' and Vince is involved in a dice game with a 'bar-fly', the replacement of Lucy Chapman. Enraged that she repeatedly picks up the dice before he tells her to, Vince presses his lighted cigarette on her hand. This clearly echoes the fate of Lucy Chapman and, in effect, tells the audience who it was who tortured her. It also fits into the dramatic pattern whereby the acts of violence against women in *The Big Heat* are cumulative in their ferocity. Lucy Chapman is tortured and killed off-screen; Katie Bannion is killed off-screen, although the blast is heard and her body is seen. The burning of the woman's hand is rendered on-screen and, of course, the culmination of this violent pattern is the scalding of Debby's face, an act which not only occurs on-screen, but whose gruesome results are later made visible.

The other motif which this scene builds on is the cold violence contained within Bannion, who witnesses the burning of the woman's hand. It will be recalled that in the Hollywood story paradigm referred to by Syd Field and others, the plot point (the narrative twist which spins the story round) towards the end of Act 2 would normally occur between pages 85 and 90. This is approximately the point in the script where the above scene in 'The Retreat' occurs. The final part of this sequence has Debby following Bannion outside and propositioning him. In fact, it marks the point where Debby's allegiance to Vince Stone begins to shift to Bannion. The fact that she becomes 'two-faced' is graphically and terrifyingly rendered in the succeeding scene in which Stone, questioning her about her involvement with Bannion, throws the boiling coffee in her face.

Bannion takes Debby back to his hotel room. Her sarcastic comment on the room – 'Say, I like this. Early nothing' – is amply reinforced by the lighting and decor, which make it as bleak and forbidding as any of the milieux of the people Bannion hunts. Bannion's hotel room is one of the film's most powerful signifiers of the extent to which he has become like those he hates. As in almost every scene in which she appears, Debby spends much of the scene looking at herself in the mirror and fixing her face. She is attracted to Bannion, but his main aim is to pump her for information about the identity of 'Larry', about which she is evasive. If Bannion is attracted to her, the attraction is overwhelmed by the coldness within him:

> DEBBY: . . . You're about as romantic as a pair of handcuffs. Didn't you ever tell a girl pretty things? You know, she's got hair like the west wind – eyes like limpid pools – skin like velvet.
>
> BANNION (hardening): I'll put you in a cab.
>
> DEBBY: Did I say something wrong?
>
> BANNION: No
>
> DEBBY: I must have broken one of the house rules. Do you really want me to go?
>
> BANNION: I wouldn't touch anything of Vince Stone's with a ten foot pole.
>
> DEBBY: That's a rotten thing to say. (Exits)

The scene in which Stone scalds Debby's face may be, as I have suggested, the main reason the film is remembered by people other than cinephiles. Shocking as it is in relation to the escalating pattern of violence against women, its *mise-en-scène* is entirely in accord with the recurrent patterns of the film. Almost as though Jerry Wald's injunction were being carried out to the letter, Debby's fascination with her own face is reprised immediately prior to the scalding – her initial

Debbie: '... a real pretty kisser'

interrogation by Stone about her whereabouts happens while she fixes her face before a mirror, and there are explicit references to her face in the dialogue. 'That's a real pretty kisser,' observes Stone as she makes up her face and lies to him. And just before seizing the coffee pot, he says, 'I'll fix you and your pretty face.' Disfigured, Debby flees back to Bannion's hotel room, the audience having learned that Lagana now wants her dead; but Bannion's continuing cold vengefulness is apparent in the dialogue between them:

> DEBBY: . . . Vince threw hot coffee in my face; I'm going to be scarred. The whole side of my face'll be scarred. (Sobs)
>
> BANNION: Where's Stone now?
>
> DEBBY: I don't know. They made Higgins take me to the doctor. (Sobs)
>
> BANNION: Higgins the Police Commissioner?
>
> DEBBY: . . . C-can I stay with you? Please can I stay? (Sobs)
>
> BANNION: I'll get you a room on this floor. Who else was with Stone?
>
> DEBBY: Gillen from the City Council. George Fuller, Vince's lawyer, and Larry Gordon. I told the doctor I didn't care what he had to do – or about the pain – only I didn't want my face scarred! (Sobs)
>
> BANNION: Who's Larry Gordon?
>
> DEBBY: You don't care! You don't care what happened to me . . . You don't care about anything or anybody. I was followed when I came here with you. That's why I got this.

The dramatic problem at this stage is to continue to push Bannion to the edge of bloody vengeance against Lagana and the mob without allowing him to cross the line which separates him from them. This is achieved through two surrogate killings, both of which, the *mise-en-scène* clearly tells us, Bannion wants to commit himself. The off-screen killing, by the mob, of Larry Gordon and the on–screen killing, by Debby, of Bertha Duncan are homologous. Bannion is in confrontation with both before their deaths and, in shots mounted in precisely the same way, strangles them almost to death. In Larry Gordon's case this is to force him to reveal all he knows about the involvement of Lagana and the mob in the death of Bannion's wife and the nature of Bertha Duncan's hold over Lagana. In a move which is on the one hand exquisitely sadistic but is, on the other hand, a mechanism whereby Bannion does not cross the line between human and hoodlum, he releases his grip on Gordon's throat and lets him know that he will spread the word that he has talked, thereby signing Gordon's death warrant.

Bannion then goes to Bertha Duncan's house and, in a shot framed precisely like the one of him with Larry Gordon, begins to strangle her. Once again Bannion is prevented from crossing the line, this time by police officers who have been warned of his visit. The killing of Bertha Duncan is, as the *mise-en-scène* tells us, a profound desire of Bannion's, especially as he now knows that her death will make public her husband's suicide letter containing the details of Lagana's operations. But the demands of the narrative, the dramatic requirement that the controlling idea of the film (that there is a line which separates decent human beings from hoodlums) must not be disavowed, mean that Bannion's impulse to kill Bertha Duncan has to be ceded to Debby. This takes place in an important scene which, like so many others in *The Big Heat* and in accordance with the best traditions of the Hollywood construct, does several things at the same time. It is the last time Bannion and Debby are together in his hotel room, and he tells her of his visit to Bertha Duncan:

BANNION: [Duncan] left her a million dollar trust fund. Wrote down everything there was to know about the Syndicate.
DEBBY: Vince must hate her insides. He never could take losing or being pressured.
BANNION: He's got to take it. If she dies, the letter goes to the newspapers. You know. I almost killed her an hour ago. I should have.
DEBBY: I don't believe you could. If you had, there wouldn't be much difference between you and Vince Stone.

Bannion's remarks here are tantamount to asking Debby to kill

Bertha Duncan. And Debby, in return, indicates her understanding of the unspoken request by restating in words the controlling idea of the film. It is morally permissible, strictly within the created universe of *The Big Heat*, for Debby to kill Bertha Duncan. Pathetic and sympathetic as she has become, she is nevertheless morally tarnished (not in terms of absolute moral judgments, but within the ethical and narrative trajectories of the film) by her previous association with Stone and Lagana. Her shifting allegiance – caught between two worlds, so to speak – is dramatically signified by her face, beautiful on one side, horrendously scarred on the other. So when Bertha Duncan comes to the door to answer Debby's ring, Debby is photographed side-on through the glass door, her 'good' profile towards the audience. In both moral and dramatic terms, she is about to enact justice on Bertha Duncan, to carry out Bannion's (and the audience's) wishes. The scene between Bertha and Debby, dressed in identical fur coats, is justly remembered:

BERTHA: Did Mr Stone send you?

Debbie's 'good' profile

DEBBY: No. I've been thinking – about you and me – how much
alike we are – the mink-coated girls.

BERTHA: I don't understand you. What are you here for, Miss
Marsh?

DEBBY: Debby – We should use first names, Bertha. We're sisters
under the mink.

BERTHA: You're not making any sense, Miss Marsh. I'd better call
Mr Stone and have him pick you up. You're not well.

DEBBY: I never felt better in my life! (Shoots Bertha).

The scene closes on the gun Debby has just fired landing on the
floor of Bertha Duncan's room. It has been a recurrent motif of this
analysis of *The Big Heat* that meaning is often carried exclusively by
cinematic means, most frequently by the dissolve. The dissolve from the
image of the gun on the floor to the next scene is one of the richest and
most complex in the film and tells us much about Bannion's innermost
impulses and feelings. The succeeding shot is of Bannion standing in the
dark street opposite Stone's apartment block and, with his back to the

Dissolve as moral comment: Bannion implicated in Mrs Duncan's murder

camera, watching Stone's arrival as reflected in a shop window. At the most obvious level of the plot, Bannion is hiding from Stone; but in the metaphorical terms clearly suggested by the dissolve, Bannion is in the dark hiding his face from the shame of instigating the act of extra-judicial killing just perpetrated by Debby. As Debby had said earlier, 'If you had killed her, there wouldn't be much difference between you and Vince Stone.' It is therefore not just for simple reasons of plot that, as Bannion faces the wall, Stone enters the frame to join him.

It is an article of faith in the screenwriting manuals not only that crises are cumulative in intensity but that the narrative should unfold in terms of gains and reversals for the central figure. It thus becomes dramatically necessary that, when Bannion appears to be making progress (as in the nailing of Larry Gordon), he should suffer a reverse. This is brought about by Lagana having Higgins remove the police guard over Bannion's daughter, and his instructions to have the child kidnapped to ensure Bannion's silence. The murder scene between Debby and Bertha Duncan and the scene it dissolves to, Bannion and Stone in the dark street, are both in their different ways about the blurring of distinctions between right and wrong, legality and criminality, i.e. local realisations of the controlling idea of the film. There is a further telling rendering of this in the scene in which Bannion, having heard of the removal of the police guard, rushes round to his brother-in-law's house and mounts the dark stairs. A figure in a hat emerges from the shadows and sticks a gun in his back. The audience immediately assumes that this is one of Lagana's men, but it turns out to be one of a number of ex-Army buddies Bannion's brother-in-law has drafted in to replace the police guard. This strategy of misdirection, the content of which restates the good/evil, legal/illegal blurring, works for two reasons. On the one hand, the audience has been led there principally because of its previous exposure to the classic Hollywood form and its consequent expectation of a reversal of fortune at this point. More particularly, however, it is the audience's previous experience of the gangster film which is being 'tapped' in order to make it read the figure coming out of the shadows as a mobster. The succeeding part of the sequence, in which Bannion meets the ex-soldiers in the apartment, is an important step in the film's reintegration of Bannion into 'normal' society.

Bannion has been waiting in the dark street outside Stone's apartment building in order to follow him upstairs. The resulting scene inside Stone's penthouse draws together the various themes and impulses of the film and effectively brings the narrative to a close. When Stone comes in, Debby, who has been waiting in the dark, throws scalding coffee in his face. In keeping with the dramatic requirement of escalating force, it is at this point that she tears off her bandage and reveals the full horror of her disfigured face to taunt Stone with what is in store for him. By the time Bannion arrives, Stone has shot Debby and, just as with Larry Gordon and Bertha Duncan, Bannion gets to the very edge of killing Stone, pointing his gun at him as Stone screams for him to shoot. Bannion lowers his gun, but even at this point it is ambiguous whether his refusal to kill Stone is because his sense of legality has reasserted itself or because of his sadistic enjoyment of Stone's pain.

It is in the scene with the dying Debby that, at one level, Bannion's reintegration into society is complete. A significant part of their earlier scenes together in his hotel room concerns his inability to speak about Katie. At this point, in response to Debby's question 'What was she like?' Bannion opens up and begins to talk about Katie. That 'the talking cure' is for him (and, of course, for the audience) and not for Debby is indicated by the fact that he goes on talking even after she dies.

Leblanc and Devismes devote considerable space to discussing the different endings of the scenario and the film itself. The original scenario ends with Bannion leaving Stone's penthouse and entering a car which will take him to have breakfast with his daughter. Clearly this is a 'happy ending' in the quite conventional sense. All Hollywood movies (certainly of this period) have a 'happy ending' in the sense that the stability/rupture/new stability structure of the classical Hollywood movie requires a new form of resolution and stasis. The ending of the film provides this, but in a highly ambiguous way which is very far indeed from the convention. Bannion is not shown being reunited with his daughter. Instead, he is reunited with the police department. He replaces his name-plate on his desk and is given a brace of freshly sharpened pencils by a uniformed colleague. The telephone rings and Bannion answers it. There has been a 'hit and run over on South Street'.

Bannion gets his coat and, with his partner, exits past a poster which reads, 'Give blood – now!'

The bleak cycle has begun once more.

CREDITS

. . . .

The Big Heat

USA
1953
Production company
Columbia Pictures
Corporation
Distributor
Columbia
Producer
Robert Arthur
Director
Fritz Lang
Screenplay
Sydney Boehm
From a *Saturday Evening Post*
serial by William P. McGivern
Photography (b & w)
Charles Lang
Music
Daniele Amfitheatrof
Musical direction
Mischa Bakaleinikoff
Editor
Charles Nelson
Art director
Robert Peterson
Set decorator
William Kiernan
Gowns
Jean Louis
Make-up
Clay Cambell
Hairstyles
Helen Hunt
Sound Engineer
George Cooper
Assistant director
Milton Feldman
90 minutes
8100 ft.

Glenn Ford
Dave Bannion
Gloria Grahame
Debby Marsh
Jocelyn Brando
Katherine 'Katie' Bannion

Alexander Scourby
Mike Lagana
Lee Marvin
Vince Stone
Jeanette Nolan
Bertha Duncan
Peter Whitney
Tierney
Willis D. Bouchey
Lt T. Wilks
Robert Burton
Gus Burke
Adam Williams
Larry Gordon
Howard Wendell
Commissioner Higgins
Chris Alcaide
George Rose
Michael Granger
Hugo
Dorothy Green
Lucy Chapman
Carolyn Jones
Doris
Ric Roman
Baldy
Dan Seymour
Atkins
Edith Evanson
Selma Parker
Norma Randall
Jill
Sid Clute
Bartender
Joe Mell
Dr Kane
Linda Bennet
Joyce
Herbert Lytton
Martin
Lyle Latell
Moving man
Ezelle Poule
Mrs Tucker
Byron Kane
Dr Jones

Mike Ross
Segal
Ted Stanhope
Butler
Phil Arnold
Nick
Bill Murphy
Reds
Douglas Evans
Gillen
Mike Mahoney
Dixon
Paul Maxey
Fuller
Pat Miller
Intern
Charles Cane
Hopkins
John Merton
Man
Kathryn Eames
Marge
Al Eben
Harry Shoenstein
William Vedder
Janitor
Harry Lauter
Hank O'Connell
Robert Forrest
Bill Rutherford
Phil Chambers
Hettrick
Jimmy Gray
Man
John Close
Policeman
John Crawford
Al
John Doucette
Mark Reiner

The print of *The Big Heat* in
the National Film Archive
was specially acquired from
Columbia-Tri-Star Pictures.

BIBLIOGRAPHY

Patrick Brantlinger, *Crusoe's Footprints: Cultural Studies in Britain and America* (New York: Routledge, 1990).

Edward Buscombe (et al.), 'Psychoanalysis and Film', in *Screen*, vol. 16 no. 4, Winter 1975–6.

Edward Buscombe (et al.), Resignation statement, in *Screen*, vol. 17 no. 2, Summer 1976.

Ian Cameron (ed.), *Movie Reader* (London: November Books, 1972).

John Caughie (ed.), *Theories of Authorship* (London: Routledge and Kegan Paul, 1981).

Jean-Luc Comolli and Paul Narboni, 'John Ford's *Young Mr Lincoln*', in *Screen*, vol. 13 no. 3, Autumn 1972.

Pam Cook (ed.), *The Cinema Book* (London: BFI, 1985).

Syd Field, *Screenplay* (New York: Delta, 1982).

Syd Field, *The Screenwriter's Workbook* (New York: Dell, 1984).

Stuart Hall and Paddy Whannel, *The Popular Arts* (London: Hutchinson, 1964).

Michael Hauge, *Writing Screenplays That Sell* (London: McGraw-Hill, 1988).

Richard Hoggart, *The Uses of Literacy* (Harmondsworth: Penguin, 1957).

Steve Jenkins, *Fritz Lang: the Image and the Look* (London: BFI, 1981).

Jim Kitses, *Horizons West* (London: Secker and Warburg/BFI, 1969).

Gérard Leblanc and Brigitte Devismes, *Le Double Scénario chez Fritz Lang* (Paris: Armand Colin, 1991).

David Lusted, Study Notes for the Slide Set from *The Big Heat* (London: BFI Education Department, 1979).

Colin McArthur, *Underworld USA* (London: Secker and Warburg/BFI, 1972).

Colin McArthur, '*Days of Hope*', in *Screen*, vol. 16 no. 4, Winter 1975–6.

Colin McArthur, *Television and History* (London: BFI, 1978).

Colin McArthur (ed.), *Scotch Reels: Scotland in Cinema and Television* (London: BFI, 1982).

Colin MacCabe, '*Days of Hope* – a response to Colin McArthur', in *Screen*, vol. 17 no. 1, Spring 1976.

William P. McGivern, *The Big Heat* (New York: Dodd Mead, 1952).

Steve Neale, *Genre* (London: BFI, 1980).

V. F. Perkins, *Film as Film* (Harmondsworth: Penguin, 1972).

Raymond Williams, *Culture and Society 1780–1950* (Harmondsworth: Penguin, 1958).

Raymond Williams, *The Long Revolution* (Harmondsworth: Penguin, 1961).

Peter Wollen, *Signs and Meaning in the Cinema* (London: Secker and Warburg/BFI, 1969, rev. ed. 1972).

Each book in the BFI Film Classics series honours a great film from the history of world cinema. With four new titles published each spring and autumn, the series will rapidly build into a collection representing some of the best writing on film. Forthcoming titles include *Citizen Kane* by Laura Mulvey, *The Big Heat* by Colin McArthur, *Brief Encounter* by Richard Dyer and *L'Atalante* by Marina Warner.

If you would like to receive further information about future BFI Film Classics or about other books on film, media and popular culture from BFI Publishing, please fill in your name and address below and return the card to the BFI.

No stamp is needed if posted in the United Kingdom, Channel Islands, or Isle of Man.

NAME

ADDRESS

POSTCODE

2

BFI Publishing
21 Stephen Street
FREEPOST 7
LONDON
W1E 4AN